68941

W9-CPB-271

B
12.
.T7132   The wisdom of Tolsto

The Wisdom of
TOLSTOY

FASKEN LEARNING RESOURCE CENTER

9000068941

68941

The Wisdom of

TOLSTOY

PHILOSOPHICAL
LIBRARY

CITADEL PRESS
Kensington Publishing Corp.
www.kensingtonbooks.com

CITADEL PRESS books are published by

Kensington Publishing Corp.
850 Third Avenue
New York, NY 10022

Copyright © 1968 Philosophical Library, Inc.

All rights reserved. No part of this book may be reproduced in any form or by any means without the prior written consent of the publisher, excepting brief quotes used in reviews.

All Kensington titles, imprints, and distributed lines are available at special quantity discounts for bulk purchases for sales promotions, premiums, fund-raising, educational, or institutional use. Special book excerpts or customized printings can also be created to fit specific needs. For details, write or phone the office of the Kensington special sales manager: Kensington Publishing Corp., 850 Third Avenue, New York, NY 10022, attn: Special Sales Department, phone 1-800-221-2647.

Citadel Press and the Citadel logo are trademarks of Kensington Publishing Corp.

First Citadel printing March 2002

10 9 8 7 6 5 4 3 2 1

Printed in the United States of America

Cataloging data for this title may be obtained from the Library of Congress.

ISBN 0-8065-2330-1

FOREWORD

Leo Nikolaevich Tolstoy was born of an aristocratic family in the Russian Province of Tula in 1828. He received a rounded education before specializing in the study of Oriental languages at the University of Kasan. At the age of 23 he entered the Army as an artillery officer and later served on the staff of a high-ranking aristocrat-general, Prince Gortschakof. Subsequently he lived in Moscow and St. Petersburg, where he led, for a short while at least, and with not too much conviction, the luxury-filled life characteristic of the idle Russian aristocracy.

By the time Tolstoy reached the age of 26 he had seen life in country and city, camp and court; he had indulged in the excesses of courtly life on the one hand, and had fought in the Battle of Sebastopol during the Crimean War on the other. It was about this time that he began to become disenchanted with life as he knew it and to seek a means of relieving the frustrations resulting from his disaffection. Thus, he turned to writing.

It was from his experience in the Battle of Sebastopol that Tolstoy first came to public awareness as a writer. The impressions he gathered from his participation in this battle were committed to paper by him under the title of *War Sketches*. When they were published in book form in 1856, he began to acquire extensive public notice. Notice became popularity during the same year with the publication of

Childhood and Youth, and popularity became nation-wide fame when, a year later, he published *The Cossacks,* a wild, romantic novel of the Steppes, drenched in realistic detail and, like all his later fiction, poetic in conception and heroically dramatic in the intensity of its execution.

The year 1860 brought the publication of *War and Peace,* a vast, historical novel dealing with the Napoleonic invasion of Russia in 1812 and the events that immediately followed the French retreat from Moscow. It was this book, above all others, that brought Tolstoy his lasting fame and assured him a place high in the hierarchy of great writers of history.

By this time Tolstoy had begun to publicly disavow the conspicuous consumption of the upper levels of Russian society of which he was, by birthright, a member. His next large work, *Anna Karenina,* was a pitiless and acerb portrayal of the vices and follies of the wealthy, aristocratic class, and praised the simplicity and unpretentious virtue of peasant life. Tolstoy's subsequent life, which was one of a country peasant leading an existence of frugality and unaffected toil in the cultivation of his land-holdings, was a result of the general conclusions he reached in the writings of *Anna Karenina.*

His decision to transform his life was based not only on his growing antipathy to the social and economic frivolousness of the society in which he lived, but on a direct and literal interpretation of the teachings of Jesus as expressed in The Sermon on the Mount.

Tolstoy's interpretation was certainly not unique in theory, but seldom if ever before had it been carried out with as much zeal, sincerity and determination. After having spent the initial thirty-five years of his life first as an accepter of the life he saw around him, then as a dissenter, then as a nihilist who could find nothing to take its place, he finally found conversion to the humanistic message of brotherliness, simplicity, and love as reflected in the teachings of Jesus. From then on, he devoted his life to championing his confidence in the natural goodness of man and to decrying the complacent indifference of the Church, rich and opulent in its trappings, to the welfare of humanity, and in so doing became somewhat of an evangelist in his determination to find in the gospels the categorical imperative of self-renunciation and brotherhood that he was to practice the rest of his days and for which he was excommunicated from the Church.

This volume is an excerpt from his *My Religion,* in which he tells the story of how he came to his awareness of the course his life should take. Let us listen to him and see if we can't find answers to some of the debilitating problems that afflict mankind today.

—Paul Rosenzweig

The Wisdom of
TOLSTOY

I

FROM my childhood, from the time I first began to read the New Testament, I was touched most of all by that portion of the doctrine of Jesus which inculcates love, humility, self-denial, and the duty of returning good for evil. This, to me, has always been the substance of Christianity; my heart recognized its truth in spite of scepticism and despair, and for this reason I submitted to a religion professed by a multitude of toilers, who find in it the solution of life,—the religion taught by the Orthodox Church. But in making my submission to the Church, I soon saw that I should not find in its creed the confirmation of the essence of Christianity; what was to me essential seemed to be in the dogma of the Church merely an accessory. What was to me the most important of the teachings of Jesus was not so regarded by the Church. No doubt (I thought) the Church sees in Christianity, aside from its inner meaning of love, humility, and self-denial, an outer, dogmatic meaning, which, however strange and even repulsive to me, is not in itself evil or pernicious. But the further I went on in submission to the doctrine of the Church, the more clearly I saw in this particular point something of greater importance than I had at first realized. What I found most repulsive in the doctrine of the Church was the strangeness of its dogmas and the approval, nay, the support, which it gave to persecutions, to the death penalty, to wars stirred up by the intolerance common to all sects; but my faith was chiefly shattered by the indifference of the Church to what seemed to me essen-

tial in the teachings of Jesus, and by its avidity for what
seemed to me of secondary importance. I felt that something was wrong; but I could not see where the fault lay, because the doctrine of the Church did not deny what seemed
to me essential in the doctrine of Jesus; this essential was
fully recognized, yet in such a way as not to give it the first
place. I could not accuse the Church of denying the essence
of the doctrine of Jesus, but it was recognized in a way
which did not satisfy me. The Church did not give me what
I expected from her. I had passed from nihilism to the
Church simply because I felt it to be impossible to live without religion, that is, without a knowledge of good and evil
beyond the animal instincts. I hoped to find this knowledge
in Christianity; but Christianity I then saw only as a vague
spiritual tendency, from which it was impossible to deduce
any clear and peremptory rules for the guidance of life.
These I sought and these I demanded of the Church. The
Church offered me rules which not only did not inculcate
the practice of the Christian life, but which made such practice still more difficult. I could not become a disciple of the
Church. An existence based upon Christian truth was to me
indispensable, and the Church only offered me rules completely at variance with the truth that I loved. The rules of
the Church touching articles of faith, dogmas, the observance of the sacrament, fasts, prayers, were not necessary to
me, and did not seem to be based on Christian truth.
Moreover, the rules of the Church weakened and sometimes destroyed the desire for Christian truth which alone
gave meaning to my life.

I was troubled most that the miseries of humanity, the
habit of judging one another, of passing judgment upon na-
tions and religions, and the wars and massacres which resulted in consequence, all went on with the approbation of
the Church. The doctrine of Jesus,—judge not, be humble,

forgive offences, deny self, love,—this doctrine was extolled by the Church in words, but at the same time the Church approved what was incompatible with the doctrine. Was it possible that the doctrine of Jesus admitted of such contradiction? I could not believe so.

Another astonishing thing about the Church was that the passages upon which it based affirmation of its dogmas were those which were most obscure. On the other hand, the passages from which came the moral laws were the most clear and precise. And yet the dogmas and the duties depending upon them were definitely formulated by the Church, while the recommendation to obey the moral law was put in the most vague and mystical terms. Was this the intention of Jesus? The Gospels alone could dissipate my doubts. I read them once and again.

Of all the other portions of the Gospels, the Sermon on the Mount always had for me an exceptional importance. I now read it more frequently than ever. Nowhere does Jesus speak with greater solemnity, nowhere does he propound moral rules more definitely and practically, nor do these rules in any other form awaken more readily an echo in the human heart; nowhere else does he address himself to a larger multitude of the common people. If there are any clear and precise Christian principles, one ought to find them here. I therefore sought the solution of my doubts in Matthew v., vi., and vii., comprising the Sermon on the Mount. These chapters I read very often, each time with the same emotional ardor, as I came to the verses which exhort the hearer to turn the other cheek, to give up his cloak, to be at peace with all the world, to love his enemies,—but each time with the same disappointment. The divine words were not clear. They exhorted to a renunciation so absolute as to entirely stifle life as I understood it; to renounce everything, therefore, could not, it seemed to me, be essential to salvation. And the moment this ceased to be an absolute condition, clearness and precision were at an end.

I read not only the Sermon on the Mount; I read all the Gospels and all the theological commentaries on the Gospels. I was not satisfied with the declarations of the theologians that the Sermon on the Mount was only an indication of the degree of perfection to which man should aspire; that man, weighed down by sin, could not reach such an ideal; and that the salvation of humanity was in faith and prayer and grace. I could not admit the truth of these propositions. It seemed to me a strange thing that Jesus should propound rules so clear and admirable, addressed to the understanding of every one, and still realize man's inability to carry his doctrine into practice.

Then as I read these maxims I was permeated with the joyous assurance that I might that very hour, that very moment, begin to practise them. The burning desire I felt led me to the attempt, but the doctrine of the Church rang in my ears,—*Man is weak, and to this he cannot attain;*—my strength soon failed. On every side I heard, "You must believe and pray"; but my wavering faith impeded prayer. Again I heard, "You must pray, and God will give you faith; this faith will inspire prayer, which in turn will invoke faith that will inspire more prayer, and so on, indefinitely." Reason and experience alike convinced me that such methods were useless. It seemed to me that the only true way was for me to try to follow the doctrine of Jesus.

And so, after all this fruitless search and careful meditation over all that had been written for and against the divinity of the doctrine of Jesus, after all this doubt and suffering, I came back face to face with the mysterious Gospel message. I could not find the meanings that others found, neither could I discover what I sought. It was only after I had rejected the interpretations of the wise critics and theologians, according to the words of Jesus, *"Except ye . . . become as little children, ye shall not enter into the kingdom of heaven"* (Matt. xviii. 3),—it was only then that I suddenly understood what had been so meaningless before. I understood, not through exegetical fantasies or profound and ingenious textual combinations; I understood everything, because I put all commentaries out of my mind. This was the passage that gave me the key to the whole:—

"Ye have heard that it hath been said, An eye for an eye, and a tooth for a tooth: But I say unto you, That ye resist not evil." (Matt. v. 38, 39.)

One day the exact and simple meaning of these words came to me; I understood that Jesus meant neither more nor less than what he said. What I saw was nothing new; only the veil that had hidden the truth from me fell away, and the truth was revealed in all its grandeur.

"Ye have heard that it hath been said, An eye for an eye, and a tooth for a tooth: But I say unto you, That ye resist not evil."

These words suddenly appeared to me as if I had never read them before. Always before, when I had read this passage, I had, singularly enough, allowed certain words to escape me, *"But I say unto you, that ye resist not evil."* To me it had always been as if the words just quoted had never existed, or had never possessed a definite meaning. Later on, as I talked with many Christians familiar with the Gospel, I noticed frequently the same blindness with regard to these words. No one remembered them, and often in speaking of this passage, Christians took up the Gospel to see for themselves if the words were really there. Through a similar neglect of these words I had failed to understand the words that follow:—

"But whosoever shall smite thee on thy right cheek, turn to him the other also," etc. (Matt. v. 39, et seq.)

Always these words had seemed to me to demand longsuffering and privation contrary to human nature. They touched me; I felt that it would be noble to follow them, but I also felt that I had not the strength to put them into practice. I said to myself, "If I turn the other cheek, I shall get another blow; if I give, all that I have will be taken away. Life would be an impossibility. Since life is given to me, why should I deprive myself of it? Jesus cannot demand as much as that." Thus I reasoned, persuaded that Jesus, in exalting long-suffering and privation, made use of exaggerated terms lacking in clearness and precision; but when I understood the words *"Resist not evil,"* I saw that Jesus did not exaggerate, that he did not demand suffering for suffering, but that he had formulated with great clearness and precision exactly what he wished to say.

"Resist not evil," knowing that you will meet with those who, when they have struck you on one cheek and met with no resistance, will strike you on the other; who, having taken away your coat, will take away your cloak also; who, having profited by your labor, will force you to labor still more without reward. And yet, though all this should happen to you, *"Resist not evil"*; do good to them that injure you. When I understood these words as they are written, all that had been obscure became clear to me, and what had seemed exaggerated I saw to be perfectly reasonable. For the first time I grasped the pivotal idea in the words *"Resist not evil"*; I saw that what followed was only a development of this command; I saw that Jesus did not exhort us to turn the other cheek that we might endure suffering, but that his exhortation was, *"Resist not evil,"* and that he afterward declared suffering to be the possible consequence of the practice of this maxim.

A father, when his son is about to set out on a far journey, commands him not to tarry by the way; he does not tell him to pass his nights without shelter, to deprive himself of food, to expose himself to rain and cold. He says, "Go thy way, and tarry not, though thou should'st be wet or cold." So Jesus does not say, "Turn the other cheek and suffer." He says, *"Resist not evil"*; no matter what happens, *"Resist not."*

These words, *"Resist not evil,"* when I understood their significance, were to me the key that opened all the rest. Then I was astonished that I had failed to comprehend words so clear and precise.

"Ye have heard that it hath been said, An eye for an eye, and a tooth for a tooth: But I say unto you, That ye resist not evil."

Whatever injury the evil-disposed may inflict upon you, bear it, give all that you have, but resist not. Could anything be more clear, more definite, more intelligible than that? I had only to grasp the simple and exact meaning of these words, just as they were spoken, when the whole doctrine of Jesus, not only as set forth in the Sermon on the Mount, but in the entire Gospels, became clear to me; what had seemed contradictory was now in harmony; above all, what had seemed superfluous was now indispensable. Each portion fell into harmonious unison and filled its proper part, like the fragments of a broken statue when adjusted in harmony with the sculptor's design. In the Sermon on the Mount, as well as throughout the whole Gospel, I found everywhere affirmation of the same doctrine, *"Resist not evil."*

In the Sermon on the Mount, as well as in many other places, Jesus represents his disciples, those who observe the rule of non-resistance to evil, as turning the other cheek, giving up their cloaks, persecuted, used despitefully, and in want. Everywhere Jesus says that he who taketh not up his cross, he who does not renounce worldly advantage, he who is not ready to bear all the consequences of the commandment, *"Resist not evil,"* cannot become his disciple.

To his disciples Jesus says, Choose to be poor; bear all

things without resistance to evil, even though you thereby bring upon yourself persecution, suffering, and death.

Prepared to suffer death rather than resist evil, he reproved the resentment of Peter, and died exhorting his followers not to resist and to remain always faithful to his doctrine. The early disciples observed this rule, and passed their lives in misery and persecution, without rendering evil for evil.

It seems, then, that Jesus meant precisely what he said. We may declare the practice of such a rule to be very difficult; we may deny that he who follows it will find happiness; we may say with the unbelievers that Jesus was a dreamer, an idealist who propounded impracticable maxims; but it is impossible not to admit that he expressed in a manner at once clear and precise what he wished to say; that is, that according to his doctrine a man must not resist evil, and, consequently, that whoever adopts his doctrine will not resist evil. And yet neither believers nor unbelievers will admit this simple and clear interpretation of Jesus' words.

II

WHEN I apprehended clearly the words *"Resist not evil,"* my conception of the doctrine of Jesus was entirely changed; and I was astounded, not that I had failed to understand it before, but that I had misunderstood it so strangely. I knew, as we all know, that the true significance of the doctrine of Jesus was comprised in the injunction to love one's neighbor. When we say, *"Turn the other cheek,"* *"Love your enemies,"* we express the very essence of Christianity. I knew all that from my childhood; but why had I failed to understand aright these simple words? Why had I always sought for some ulterior meaning? *"Resist not evil"* means, never resist, never oppose violence; or, in other words, never do anything contrary to the law of love. If any one takes advantage of this disposition and affronts you, bear the affront, and do not, above all, have recourse to violence. This Jesus said in words so clear and simple that it would be impossible to express the idea more clearly. How was it then, that believing or trying to believe these to be the words of God, I still maintained the impossibility of obeying them? If my master says to me, "Go; cut some wood," and I reply, "It is beyond my strength," I say one of two things: either I do not believe what my master says, or I do not wish to obey his commands. Should I then say of God's commandment that I could not obey it without the aid of a supernatural power? Should I say this without having made the slightest effort of my own to obey? We are told that God descended to earth to save mankind; that salvation was secured by the second person of the Trinity, who suffered for men, thereby redeeming them from sin, and gave them the Church as the shrine for the transmission of grace to all believers; but aside from this, the Saviour gave to men a doctrine and the example of his own life for their salvation. How, then, could I say that the rules of life which Jesus has formulated so clearly and simply for every one— how could I say that these rules were difficult to obey, that it was impossible to obey them without the assistance of a supernatural power? Jesus saw no such impossibility; he distinctly declared that those who did not obey could not enter into the kingdom of God. Nowhere did he say that obedience would be difficult; on the contrary, he said in so many words, *"My yoke is easy and my burden is light"* (Matt. xi. 30). And John, the evangelist, says, *"His commandments are not grievous"* (1 John v. 3). Since God declared the practice of his law to be easy, and himself practised it in human form, as did also his disciples, how dared I speak of the impossibility of obedience without the aid of a supernatural power?

If one bent all his energies to overthrow any law, what could he say of greater force than that the law was essentially impracticable, and that the maker of the law knew it to be impracticable and unattainable without the aid of a supernatural power? Yet that is exactly what I had been thinking of the command, *"Resist not evil."* I endeavored to find out how it was that I got the idea that Jesus' law was divine, but that it could not be obeyed; and as I reviewed my past history, I perceived that the idea had not been communicated to me in all its crudeness (it would then have been revolting to me), but insensibly I had been imbued with it from childhood, and all my after life had only confirmed me in error.

From my childhood I had been taught that Jesus was

God, and that his doctrine was divine, but at the same time I was taught to respect as sacred the institutions which protected me from violence and evil. I was taught to resist evil, that it was humiliating to submit to evil, and that resistance to it was praiseworthy. I was taught to judge, and to inflict punishment. Then I was taught the soldier's trade, that is, to resist evil by homicide; the army to which I belonged was called "The Christophile Army," and it was sent forth with a Christian benediction. From infancy to manhood I learned to venerate things that were in direct contradiction to the law of Jesus,—to meet an aggressor with his own weapons, to avenge myself by violence for all offences against my person, my family, or my race. Not only was I not blamed for this; I learned to regard it as not at all contrary to the law of Jesus. All that surrounded me, my personal security and that of my family and my property—depended then upon a law which Jesus reproved,—the law of "a tooth for a tooth." My spiritual instructors taught me that the law of Jesus was divine, but, because of human weakness, impossible of practice, and that the grace of Jesus Christ alone could aid us to follow its precepts. And this instruction agreed with what I received in secular institutions and from the social organization about me. I was so thoroughly possessed with this idea of the impracticability of the divine doctrine, the idea conformed so well with my desires, that not till the time of awakening did I realize its falsity. I did not see how impossible it was to confess Jesus and his doctrine, *"Resist not evil,"* and at the same time deliberately assist in the organization of property, of tribunals, of governments, of armies; to contribute to the establishment of a polity entirely contrary to the doctrine of Jesus, and at the same time pray to Jesus to help us to obey his commands, to forgive our sins, and to aid us that we resist not evil. I did not see, what is very clear to me now, how much more simple it would be to organize a method of living conformable to the law of Jesus, and then to pray for tribunals, and massacres, and wars, if these things were indispensable to our happiness.

Thus I came to understand the source of error into which I had fallen. I had confessed Jesus with my lips, but my heart was still far from him. The command, *"Resist not evil,"* is the central point of Jesus' doctrine; it is not a mere verbal affirmation; it is a rule whose practice is obligatory. It is verily the key to the whole mystery; but the key must be thrust to the bottom of the lock. When we regard it as a command impossible of performance, the value of the entire doctrine is lost. Why should not a doctrine seem impracticable, when we have suppressed its fundamental proposition? It is not strange that unbelievers look upon it as totally absurd. When we declare that one may be a Christian without observing the commandment, *"Resist not evil,"* we simply leave out the connecting link which transmits the force of the doctrine of Jesus into action.

Some time ago I was reading in Hebrew, the fifth chapter of Matthew with a Jewish rabbi. At nearly every verse the rabbi said, "This is in the Bible," or "This is in the Talmud," and he showed me in the Bible and in the Talmud sentences very like the declarations of the Sermon on the Mount. When we reached the words, *"Resist not evil,"* the rabbi did not say, "This is in the Talmud," but he asked me, with a smile, "Do the Christians obey this command? Do they turn the other cheek?" I had nothing to say in reply, especially as at that particular time, Christians, far from turning the other cheek, were smiting the Jews upon both cheeks. I asked him if there were anything similar in the Bible or in the Talmud. "No," he replied, "there is nothing like it; but tell me, do the Christians obey this law?" It was only another way of saying that the presence in the Christian doctrine of a commandment which no one observed, and which Christians themselves regarded as impracticable, is simply an avowal of the foolishness and nullity of that law. I could say nothing in reply to the rabbi.

Now that I understand the exact meaning of the doctrine, I see clearly the strangely contradictory position in which I was placed. Having recognized the divinity of Jesus and of his doctrine, and having at the same time organized a life wholly contrary to that doctrine, what remained for me but to look upon the doctrine as impracticable? In words I had recognized the doctrine of Jesus as sacred; in actions, I had professed a doctrine not at all Christian, and I had recognized and reverenced the anti-Christian customs which hampered my life upon every side. The persistent message of the Old Testament is that misfortunes came upon the Hebrew people because they believed in false gods and denied Jehovah. Samuel (I. viii.–xii.) accuses the people of adding to their other apostasies the choice of a man, upon whom they depended for deliverance instead of upon Jehovah, who was their true King. "Turn not aside after *tohu*, after vain things," Samuel says to the people (I. xii. 21); "turn not aside after vain things, which cannot profit nor deliver; for they are *tohu*, are vain." "Fear Jehovah and serve him. . . . But if ye shall still do wickedly, ye shall be consumed, both ye and your king" (I. xii. 24, 25). And so with me, faith in *tohu*, in vain things, in empty idols, had concealed the truth from me. Across the path which led to the truth, *tohu*, the idol of vain things, rose before me, cutting off the light, and I had not the strength to beat it down.

On a certain day, at this time, I was walking in Moscow towards the Borovitzky Gate, where was stationed an old lame beggar, with a dirty cloth wrapped about his head. I took out my purse to bestow an alms; but at the same moment I saw a young soldier emerging from the Kremlin at a rapid pace, head well up, red of face, wearing the State in-signia of military dignity. The beggar, on perceiving the sol-dier, arose in fear, and ran with all his might towards the Alexander Garden. The soldier, after a vain attempt to come up with the fugitive, stopped, shouting forth an impreca-tion upon the poor wretch who had established himself under the gateway contrary to regulations. I waited for the soldier. When he approached me, I asked him if he knew how to read.

"Yes; why do you ask?"

"Have you read the New Testament?"

"Yes."

"And do you remember the words, 'If thine enemy hunger, feed him. . .'?"

I repeated the passage. He remembered it, and heard me to the end. I saw that he was uneasy. Two passers-by stopped and listened. The soldier seemed to be troubled that he should be condemned for doing his duty in driving persons away from a place where they had been forbidden to linger. He thought himself at fault, and sought for an ex-cuse.

Suddenly his eye brightened; he looked at me over his shoulder, as if he were about to move away.

"And the military regulation, do you know anything about that?" he demanded.

"No," I said.

"In that case, you have nothing to say to me," he retorted, with a triumphant wag of the head, and elevating his plume once more, he marched away to his post. He was the only man that I ever met who had solved, with an inflexible logic, the question which eternally confronted me in social relations, and which rises continually before every man who calls himself a Christian.

III

WE are wrong when we say that the Christian doctrine is concerned only with the salvation of the individual, and has nothing to do with questions of State. Such an assertion is simply a bold affirmation of an untruth, which, when we examine it seriously, falls of itself to the ground. It is well (so I said); I will resist not evil; I will turn the other cheek in private life; but hither comes the enemy, or here is an oppressed nation, and I am called upon to do my part in the struggle against evil, to go forth and kill. I must decide the question, to serve God or *tohu*, to go to war or not to go. Perhaps I am a peasant; I am appointed mayor of a village, a judge, a juryman; I am obliged to take the oath of office, to judge, to condemn. What ought I to do? Again I must choose between the divine law and the human law. Perhaps I am a monk living in a monastery; the neighboring peasants trespass upon our pasturage, and I am appointed to resist evil, to plead for justice against the wrong-doers. Again I must choose. It is a dilemma from which no man can escape.

I do not speak of those whose entire lives are passed in resisting evil, as military authorities, judges, or governors. No one is so obscure that he is not obliged to choose between the service of God and the service of *tohu*, in his relation to the State. My very existence, entangled with that of the State and the social existence organized by the State, exacts from me an anti-Christian activity directly contrary to the commandments of Jesus. In fact, with conscription and compulsory jury service, this pitiless dilemma arises before every one. Every one is forced to take up murderous weapons; and even if he does not get as far as murder, his weapons must be ready, his carbine loaded, and his sword keen of edge, that he may declare himself ready for murder. Every one is forced into the service of the courts to take part in meting out judgment and sentence; that is, to deny the commandment of Jesus, *"Resist not evil,"* in acts as well as in words.

The soldier's problem, the Gospel or military regulations, divine law or human law, is before mankind to-day as it was in the time of Samuel. It was forced upon Jesus and upon his disciples; it is forced in these times upon all who would be Christians; and it was forced upon me.

The law of Jesus, with its doctrine of love, humility, and self-denial, touched my heart more deeply than ever before. But everywhere, in the annals of history, in the events that were going on about me, in my individual life, I saw the law opposed in a manner revolting to sentiment, conscience, and reason, and encouraging to brute instincts. I felt that if I adopted the law of Jesus, I should be alone; I should pass many unhappy hours; I should be persecuted and afflicted as Jesus had said. But if I adopted the human law, everybody would approve; I should be in peace and safety, with all the resources of civilization at my command to put my conscience at ease. As Jesus said, I should laugh and be glad. I felt all this, and so I did not analyze the meaning of the doctrine of Jesus, but sought to understand it in such a way that it might not interfere with my life as an animal. That is, I did not wish to understand it at all. This determination not to understand led me into delusions which now astound me. As an instance in point, let me explain my former understanding of these words:—

"Judge not, that ye be not judged." (Matt. vii. 1.)

"Judge not, and ye shall not be judged; condemn not, and ye shall not be condemned." (Luke vi. 37.)

The courts in which I served, and which insured the safety of my property and my person, seemed to be institutions so indubitably sacred and so entirely in accord with the divine law, it had never entered into my head that the words I have quoted could have any other meaning than an injunction not to speak ill of one's neighbor. It never occurred to me that Jesus spoke in these words of the courts of human law and justice. It was only when I understood the true meaning of the words, *"Resist not evil,"* that the question arose as to Jesus' advice with regard to tribunals. When I understood that Jesus would denounce them, I asked myself, Is not this the real meaning: Not only do not judge your neighbor, do not speak ill of him, but do not judge him in the courts, do not judge him in any of the tribunals that you have instituted? Now in Luke (vi. 37–49) these words follow immediately the doctrine that exhorts us to resist not evil and to do good to our enemies. And after the injunction, *"Be ye therefore merciful, as your Father also is merciful,"* Jesus says, *"Judge not, and ye shall not be judged; condemn not, and ye shall not be condemned."* *"Judge not;"* does not this mean, Institute no tribunals for the judgment of your neighbor? I had only to bring this boldly before myself when heart and reason united in an affirmative reply.

To show how far I was before from the true interpretation, I shall confess a foolish pleasantry for which I still blush. When I was reading the New Testament as a divine book at the time that I had become a believer, I was in the habit of saying to my friends who were judges or attorneys, "And you still judge, although it is said, 'Judge not, and ye shall not be judged'?" I was so sure that these words could have no other meaning than a condemnation of evil-speaking that I did not comprehend the horrible blasphemy which I thus committed. I was so thoroughly convinced that these words did not mean what they did mean, that I quoted them in their true sense in the form of a pleasantry.

I shall relate in detail how it was that all doubt with regard to the true meaning of these words was effaced from my mind, and how I saw their purport to be that Jesus denounced the institution of all human tribunals, of whatever sort; that he meant to say so, and could not have expressed himself otherwise. When I understood the command, *"Resist not evil,"* in its proper sense, the first thing that occurred to me was that tribunals, instead of conforming to this law, were directly opposed to it, and indeed to the entire doctrine; and therefore that if Jesus had thought of tribunals at all, he would have condemned them.

Jesus said, *"Resist not evil"*; the sole aim of tribunals is to resist evil. Jesus exhorted us to return good for evil; tribunals return evil for evil. Jesus said that we were to make no distinction between those who do good and those who do evil; tribunals do nothing else. Jesus said, Forgive, forgive not once or seven times, but without limit; love your enemies, do good to them that hate you—but tribunals do not forgive, they punish; they return not good but evil to those whom they regard as the enemies of society. It would seem, then, that Jesus denounced judicial institutions. Perhaps (I said) Jesus never had anything to do with courts of justice, and so did not think of them. But I saw that such a theory was not tenable. Jesus, from his childhood to his death, was concerned with the tribunals of Herod, of the Sanhedrim, and of the High Priests. I saw that Jesus must have regarded courts of justice as wrong. He told his disciples that they would be dragged before the judges, and gave them advice as to how they should comport themselves. He said of himself that he should be condemned by a tribunal, and he showed what the attitude toward judges ought to be. Jesus, then, must have thought of the judicial institutions which condemned him and his disciples; which have condemned and continue to condemn millions of men.

Jesus saw the wrong and faced it. When the sentence against the woman taken in adultery was about to be carried into execution, he absolutely denied the possibility of human justice, and demonstrated that man could not be the judge since man himself was guilty. And this idea he has propounded many times, as where it is declared that one with a beam in his eye cannot see the mote in another's eye, or that the blind cannot lead the blind. He even pointed out the consequences of such misconceptions,—the disciple would be above his Master.

Perhaps, however, after having denounced the incompetency of human justice as displayed in the case of the woman taken in adultery, or illustrated in the parable of the mote and the beam; perhaps, after all, Jesus would admit of an appeal to the justice of men where it was necessary for protection against evil; but I soon saw that this was inadmissible. In the Sermon on the Mount, he says, addressing the multitude,

"And if any man will sue thee at the law, and take away thy coat, let him have thy cloak also." (Matt. v. 40.)

Once more, perhaps Jesus spoke only of the personal bearing which a man should have when brought before judicial institutions, and did not condemn justice, but admitted the necessity in a Christian society of individuals who judge others in properly constituted forms. But I saw that this view was also inadmissible. When he prayed, Jesus besought all men, without exception, to forgive others, that their own trespasses might be forgiven. This thought he often expresses. He who brings his gift to the altar with prayer must first grant forgiveness. How, then, could a man

judge and condemn when his religion commanded him to
forgive all trespasses, without limit? So I saw that according
to the doctrine of Jesus no Christian judge could pass sentence of condemnation.

But might not the relation between the words *"Judge not,
and ye shall not be judged"* and the preceding or subsequent
passages permit us to conclude that Jesus, in saying *"Judge
not,"* had no reference whatever to judicial institutions? No;
this could not be so; on the contrary, it is clear from the relation of the phrases that in saying *"Judge not,"* Jesus did actually speak of judicial institutions. According to Matthew
and Luke, before saying *"Judge not, condemn not,"* his command was to resist not evil. And prior to this, as Matthew
tells us, he repeated the ancient criminal law of the Jews,
"An eye for an eye, and a tooth for a tooth." Then, after this reference to the old criminal law, he added, *"But I say unto you,
That ye resist not evil"*; and, after that, *"Judge not."* Jesus did,
then, refer directly to human criminal law, and reproved it
in the words, *"Judge not."* Moreover, according to Luke, he
not only said, *"Judge not,"* but also, *"Condemn not."* It was
not without a purpose that he added this almost synony-
mous word; it shows clearly what meaning should be at-
tributed to the other. If he had wished to say "Judge not
your neighbor," he would have said "neighbor"; but he
added the words which are translated *"Condemn not,"* and
then completed the sentence, *"And ye shall not be condemned:
forgive, and ye shall be forgiven."* But some may still insist that
Jesus, in expressing himself in this way, did not refer at all
to the tribunals, and that I have read my own thoughts into
his teachings. Let the apostles tell us what they thought of
courts of justice, and if they recognized and approved of
them. The apostle James says (iv. 11, 12):—

*"Speak not evil one of another, brethren. He that speaketh evil
of his brother, and judgeth his brother, speaketh evil of the law,*

and judgeth the law: but if thou judge the law, thou art not a doer of the law, but a judge. There is one lawgiver, who is able to save and to destroy: who art thou that judgest another?"

The word translated "speak evil" is the verb καταλαλέω, which means "to speak against, to accuse"; this is its true meaning, as any one may find out for himself by opening a dictionary. In the translation we read, *"He that speaketh evil of his brother, . . . speaketh evil of the law."* Why so? is the question that involuntarily arises. I may speak evil of my brother, but I do not thereby speak evil of the law. If, however, I *accuse* my brother, if I bring him to justice, it is plain that I thereby accuse the law of Jesus of insufficiency: I accuse and judge the law. It is clear, then, that I do not practise the law, but that I make myself a judge of the law. *"Not to judge, but to save"* is Jesus' declaration. How then shall I, who cannot save, become a judge and punish? The entire passage refers to human justice, and denies its authority. The whole epistle is permeated with the same idea. In the second chapter we read:—

"For he shall have judgment without mercy, that hath shewed no mercy; and mercy is exalted above judgment."[1] (Jas. ii. 13.)

(The last phrase has been translated in such a way as to declare that judgment is compatible with Christianity, but that it ought to be merciful.)

James exhorts his brethren to have no respect of persons. If you have respect of the condition of persons, you are guilty of sin; you are like the untrustworthy judges of the tribunals. You look upon the beggar as the refuse of society, while it is the rich man who ought to be so regarded. He it is who oppresses you and draws you before the judgment-seats. If you live according to the law of love for your neighbor, according to the law of mercy (which James calls *"the*

---

[1]Count Tolstoi's rendering.

law of liberty," to distinguish it from all others)—if you live according to this law, it is well. But if you have respect of persons, you transgress the law of mercy. Then (doubtless thinking of the case of the woman taken in adultery, who, when she was brought before Jesus, was about to be put to death according to the law), thinking, no doubt, of that case, James says that he who inflicts death upon the adulterous woman would himself be guilty of murder, and thereby transgress the eternal law; for the same law forbids both adultery and murder.

"So speak ye, and so do, as they that shall be judged by the law of liberty. For he shall have judgment without mercy, that hath shewed no mercy; and mercy is exalted above judgment." (Jas. ii. 12, 13.)

Could the idea be expressed in terms more clear and precise? Respect of persons is forbidden, as well as any judgment that shall classify persons as good or bad; human judgment is declared to be inevitably defective, and such judgment is denounced as criminal when it condemns for crime; judgment is blotted out by the eternal law, the law of mercy.

I open the epistles of Paul, who had been a victim of tribunals, and in the letter to the Romans I read the admonitions of the apostle for the vices and errors of those to whom his words are addressed; among other matters he speaks of courts of justice:—

"Who, knowing the judgment of God, that they which commit such things are worthy of death, not only do the same, but have pleasure in them that do them." (Rom. i. 32.)

"Therefore thou art inexcusable, O man, whosoever thou art that judgest: for wherein thou judgest another, thou condemnest thyself; for thou that judgest doest the same things." (Rom. ii. 1.)

"Or despisest thou the riches of his goodness and forbearance

and longsuffering; not knowing that the goodness of God leadeth thee to repentance?" (Rom. ii. 4.)

Such was the opinion of the apostles with regard to tri-bunals, and we know that human justice was among the tri-als and sufferings that they endured with steadfastness and resignation to the will of God. When we think of the situa-tion of the early Christians, surrounded by unbelievers, we can understand the futility of denying to tribunals the right to judge persecuted Christians. The apostles spoke casually of tribunals as grievous, and denied their authority on every occasion.

I examined the teachings of the early Fathers of the Church, and found them to agree in obliging no one to judge or to condemn, and in urging all to bear the inflic-tions of justice. The martyrs, by their acts, declared them-selves to be of the same mind. I saw that Christianity before Constantine regarded tribunals only as an evil which was to be endured with patience; but it never could have occurred to any early Christian that he could take part in the admin-istration of the courts of justice. It is plain, therefore, that Jesus' words, *"Judge not, condemn not,"* were understood by his first disciples, as they ought to be understood now, in their direct and literal meaning: judge not in courts of jus-tice; take no part in them.

All this seemed absolutely to corroborate my conviction that the words, *"Judge not, condemn not,"* referred to the jus-tice of tribunals. Yet the meaning, "Speak not evil of your neighbor," is so firmly established, and courts of justice flaunt their decrees with so much assurance and audacity in all Christian societies, with the support even of the Church, that for a long time still I doubted the wisdom of my inter-pretation. If men have understood the words in this way (I thought), and have instituted Christian tribunals, they must certainly have some reason for so doing; there must be a good reason for regarding these words as a denunciation of evil-speaking, and there is certainly a basis of some sort for the institution of Christian tribunals; perhaps, after all, I am in the wrong.

I turned to the Church commentaries. In all, from the fifth century onward, I found the invariable interpretation to be, "Accuse not your neighbor"; that is, avoid evil-speaking. As the words came to be understood exclusively in this sense, a difficulty arose,—How to refrain from judgment? It being impossible not to condemn evil, all the commentators discussed the question, What is blamable and what is not blamable? Some, such as Chrysostom and Theophylact, said that, as far as servants of the Church were concerned, the phrase could not be construed as a prohibition of censure, since the apostles themselves were censorious. Others said that Jesus doubtless referred to the Jews, who accused their neighbors of shortcomings, and were themselves guilty of great sins.

Nowhere a word about human institutions, about tribunals, to show how they were affected by the warning, *"Judge not."* Did Jesus sanction courts of justice, or did he not? To this very natural question I found no reply—as if it was evident that from the moment a Christian took his seat on the judge's bench he might not only judge his neighbor, but condemn him to death.

I turned to other writers, Greek, Catholic, Protestant, to the Tübingen school, to the historical school. Everywhere, even by the most liberal commentators, the words in question were interpreted as an injunction against evil-speaking.

But why, contrary to the spirit of the whole doctrine of Jesus, are these words interpreted in so narrow a way as to exclude courts of justice from the injunction, *"Judge not"*?

Why the supposition that Jesus in forbidding the comparatively light offence of speaking evil of one's neighbor did not forbid, did not even consider, the more deliberate judgment which results in punishment inflicted upon the condemned? To all this I got no response; not even an allusion to the least possibility that the words "to judge" could be used as referring to a court of justice, to the tribunals from whose punishments so many millions have suffered.

Moreover, when the words, *"Judge not, condemn not,"* are under discussion, the cruelty of judging in courts of justice is passed over in silence, or else commended. The commentators all declare that in Christian societies tribunals are necessary, and in no way contrary to the law of Jesus.

Realizing this, I began to doubt the sincerity of the commentators; and I did what I should have done in the first place; I turned to the textual translations of the words which we render "to judge" and "to condemn." In the original these words are κρίνω and καταδικάζω. The defective translation in James of καταλαλέω, which is rendered "to speak evil," strengthened my doubts as to the correct translation of the others. When I looked through different versions of the Gospels, I found καταδικάζω rendered in the Vulgate by *condemnare*, "to condemn"; in the Slavonian text the rendering is equivalent to that of the Vulgate; Luther has *verdammen*, "to speak evil of." These divergent renderings increased my doubts, and I was obliged to ask again the meaning of κρίνω, as used by the two evangelists, and of καταδικάζω, as used by Luke who, scholars tell us, wrote very correct Greek.

How would these words be translated by a man who knew nothing of the evangelical creed, and who had before him only the phrases in which they are used?

Consulting the dictionary, I found that the word κρίνω had several different meanings, among the most used being "to condemn in a court of justice," and even "to condemn to death," but in no instance did it signify "to speak evil." I consulted a dictionary of New Testament Greek, and found that was often used in the sense "to condemn in a court of justice," sometimes in the sense "to choose," never as meaning "to speak evil." From which I inferred that the word κρίνω might be translated in different ways, but that the rendering "to speak evil" was the most forced and far-fetched.

I searched for the word καταδικάζω, which follows κρίνω, evidently to define more closely the sense in which the latter is to be understood. I looked for καταδικάζω in the dictionary, and found that it had no other signification than "to condemn in judgment," or "to judge worthy of death." I found that the word was used four times in the New Testament, each time in the sense "to condemn under sentence, to judge worthy of death." In James (v. 6) we read, *"Ye have condemned and killed the just."* The word rendered "condemned" is this same καταδικάζω, and is used with reference to Jesus, who was condemned to death by a court of justice. The word is never used in any other sense, in the New Testament or in any other writing in the Greek language.

What, then, are we to say to all this? Is my conclusion a foolish one? Is not every one who considers the fate of humanity filled with horror at the sufferings inflicted upon mankind by the enforcement of criminal codes,—a scourge to those who condemn as well as to the condemned,—from the slaughters of Genghis Khan to those of the French Revolution and the executions of our own times? He would indeed be without compassion who could refrain from feeling horror and repulsion, not only at the sight of human beings thus treated by their kind, but at the simple recital of death inflicted by the knout, the guillotine, or the gibbet.

The Gospel, of which every word is sacred to you, de-clares distinctly and without equivocation: "You have from of old a criminal law, An eye for an eye, a tooth for a tooth; but a new law is given you, That you resist not evil. Obey this law; render not evil for evil, but do good to every one, forgive every one, under all circumstances." Further on comes the injunction, *"Judge not,"* and that these words might not be misunderstood, Jesus added, *"Condemn not; condemn not in justice the crimes of others."*

"No more death-warrants," said an inner voice—"no more death-warrants," said the voice of science; "evil can-not suppress evil." The Word of God, in which I believed, told me the same thing. And when in reading the doctrine, I came to the words, *"Condemn not, and ye shall not be con-demned: forgive, and ye shall be forgiven,"* could I look upon them as meaning simply that I was not to indulge in gossip and evil-speaking, and should continue to regard tribunals as a Christian institution, and myself as a Christian judge?

I was overwhelmed with horror at the grossness of the error into which I had fallen.

IV

I NOW understood the words of Jesus: *"Ye have heard that it hath been said, An eye for an eye, and a tooth for a tooth: but I say unto you, That ye resist not evil."* Jesus' meaning is: "You have thought that you were acting in a reasonable manner in defending yourself by violence against evil, in tearing out an eye for an eye, by fighting against evil with criminal tribunals, guardians of the peace, armies; but I say unto you, Renounce violence; have nothing to do with violence; do harm to no one, not even to your enemy." I understood now that in saying *"Resist not evil,"* Jesus not only told us what would result from the observance of this rule, but established a new basis for society conformable to his doctrine and opposed to the social basis established by the law of Moses, by Roman law, and by the different codes in force to-day. He formulated a new law whose effect would be to deliver humanity from its self-indicted woes. His declaration was: "You believe that your laws reform criminals; as a matter of fact, they only make more criminals. There is only one way to suppress evil, and that is to return good for evil, without respect of persons. For thousands of years you have tried the other method; now try mine, try the reverse."

Strange to say, in these later days, I talked with different persons about this commandment of Jesus, *"Resist not evil,"* and rarely found any one to coincide with my opinion! Two classes of men would never, even by implication, admit the literal interpretation of the law. These men were at the extreme poles of the social scale,—they were the conservative

Christian patriots who maintained the infallibility of the
Church, and the atheistic revolutionists. Neither of these
two classes was willing to renounce the right to resist by violence what they regarded as evil. And the wisest and most
intelligent among them would not acknowledge the simple
and evident truth, that if we once admit the right of any
man to resist by violence what he regards as evil, every
other man has equally the right to resist by violence what
he regards as evil.

Not long ago I had in my hands an interesting correspon-
dence between an orthodox Slavophile and a Christian rev-
olutionist. The one advocated violence as a partisan of a
war for the relief of brother Slavs in bondage; the other, as a
partisan of revolution, in the name of our brothers the oppressed Russian peasantry. Both invoked violence, and
each based himself upon the doctrine of Jesus. The doctrine
of Jesus is understood in a hundred different ways; but
never, unhappily, in the simple and direct way which har-
monizes with the inevitable meaning of Jesus' words.

Our entire social fabric is founded upon principles that
Jesus reproved; we do not wish to understand his doctrine
in its simple and direct acceptation, and yet we assure ourselves and others that we follow his doctrine, or else that
his doctrine is not expedient for us. Believers profess that
Christ as God, the second person of the Trinity, descended
upon earth to teach men by his example how to live; they
go through the most elaborate ceremonies for the consum-
mation of the sacraments, the building of temples, the send-
ing out of missionaries, the establishment of priesthoods,
for parochial administration, for the performance of rituals;
but they forget one little detail,—the practice of the commandments of Jesus. Unbelievers endeavor in every possible way to organize their existence independent of the
doctrine of Jesus, they having decided *a priori* that this doc-

trine is of no account. But to endeavor to put his teachings in practice, this each refuses to do; and the worst of it is, that without any attempt to put them in practice, both believers and unbelievers decide *a priori* that it is impossible.

Jesus said, simply and clearly, that the law of resistance to evil by violence, which has been made the basis of society, is false, and contrary to man's nature; and he gave another basis, that of nonresistance to evil, a law which, according to his doctrine, would deliver man from wrong. "You believe" (he says in substance) "that your laws, which resort to violence, correct evil; not at all; they only augment it. For thousands of years you have tried to destroy evil by evil, and you have not destroyed it; you have only augmented it. Do as I command you, follow my example, and you will know that my doctrine is true." Not only in words, but by his acts, by his death, did Jesus propound his doctrine, *"Resist not evil."*

Believers listen to all this. They hear it in their churches, persuaded that the words are divine; they worship Jesus as God, and then they say: "All this is admirable, but it is impossible; as society is now organized, it would derange our whole existence, and we should be obliged to give up the customs that are so dear to us. We believe it all, but only in this sense: That it is the ideal toward which humanity ought to move; the ideal which is to be attained by prayer, and by believing in the sacraments, in the redemption, and in the resurrection of the dead."

The others, the unbelievers, the free-thinkers who comment on the doctrine of Jesus, the historians of religions, the Strausses, the Renans,—completely imbued with the teachings of the Church, which says that the doctrine of Jesus accords with difficulty with our conceptions of life,—tell us very seriously that the doctrine of Jesus is the doctrine of a visionary, the consolation of feeble minds; that it was all

very well preached in the fishermen's huts by Galilee; but
that for us it is only the sweet dream of one whom Renan
calls the "charmant docteur."

In their opinion, Jesus could not rise to the heights of
wisdom and culture attained by our civilization. If he had
been on an intellectual level with his modern critics, he
never would have uttered his charming nonsense about the
birds of the air, the turning of the other cheek, the taking no
thought for the morrow. These historical critics judge of the
value of Christianity by what they see of it as it now exists.
The Christianity of our age and civilization approves of society as it now is, with its prison-cells, its factories, its
houses of infamy, its parliaments; but as for the doctrine of
Jesus, which is opposed to modern society, it is only empty
words. The historical critics see this, and, unlike the so-
called believers, having no motives for concealment, submit
the doctrine to a careful analysis; they refute it systemati-
cally, and prove that Christianity is made up of nothing but
chimerical ideas.

It would seem that before deciding upon the doctrine of
Jesus, it would be necessary to understand of what it consisted; and to decide whether his doctrine is reasonable or
not, it would be well first to realize that he said exactly
what he did say. And this is precisely what we do not do,
what the Church commentators do not do, what the free-
thinkers do not do—and we know very well why. We know
perfectly well that the doctrine of Jesus is directed at and
denounces all human errors, all *tohu*, all the empty idols
that we try to except from the category of errors, by dub-
bing them "Church," "State," "Culture," "Science," "Art,"
"Civilization." But Jesus spoke precisely of all these, of
these and all other *tohu*. Not only Jesus, but all the Hebrew
prophets, John the Baptist, all the true sages of the world

denounced the Church and State and culture and civilization of their times as sources of man's perdition.

Imagine an architect who says to a house-owner, "Your house is good for nothing; you must rebuild it," and then describes how the supports are to be cut and fastened. The proprietor turns a deaf ear to the words, "Your house is good for nothing," and only listens respectfully when the architect begins to discuss the arrangement of the rooms. Evidently, in this case, all the subsequent advice of the architect will seem to be impracticable; less respectful proprietors would regard it as nonsensical. But it is precisely in this way that we treat the doctrine of Jesus. I give this illustration for want of a better. I remember now that Jesus in teaching his doctrine made use of the same comparison. *"Destroy this temple,"* he said, *"and in three days I will raise it up."* It was for this they put him on the cross, and for this they now crucify his doctrine.

The least that can be asked of those who pass judgment upon any doctrine is that they shall judge of it with the same understanding as that with which it was propounded. Jesus understood his doctrine, not as a vague and distant ideal impossible of attainment, not as a collection of fantastic and poetical reveries with which to charm the simple inhabitants on the shores of Galilee; to him his doctrine was a doctrine of action, of acts which should become the salvation of mankind. This he showed in his manner of applying his doctrine. The crucified one who cried out in agony of spirit and died for his doctrine was not a dreamer; he was a man of action. They are not dreamers who have died, and still die, for his doctrine. No; that doctrine is not a chimera!

All doctrine that reveals the truth is chimerical to the blind. We may say, as many people do say (I was of the number), that the doctrine of Jesus is chimerical because it is contrary to human nature. It is against nature, we say, to turn the other cheek when we have been struck, to give all that we possess, to toil, not for ourselves, but for others. It is natural, we say, for a man to defend his person, his family, his property; that is to say, it is the nature of man to struggle for existence. A learned person has proved scientifically that the most sacred duty of man is to defend his rights, that is, to fight.

But the moment we detach ourselves from the idea that the existing organization established by man is the best, is sacred, the moment we do this, the objection that the doctrine of Jesus is contrary to human nature turns immediately upon him who makes it. No one will deny that not only to kill or torture a man, but to torture a dog, to kill a fowl or calf, is to inflict suffering reproved by human nature. (I have known of farmers who had ceased to eat meat solely because it had fallen to their lot to slaughter animals.) And yet our existence is so organized that every personal enjoyment is purchased at the price of human suffering contrary to human nature.

We have only to examine closely the complicated mechanism of our institutions that are based upon coercion to realize that coercion and violence are contrary to human nature. The judge who has condemned according to the code, is not willing to hang the criminal with his own hands; no clerk would tear a villager from his weeping family and cast him into prison; the general or the soldier, unless he be hardened by discipline and service, will not undertake to slay a hundred Turks or Germans or destroy a village, would not, if he could help it, kill a single man. Yet all these things are done, thanks to the administrative machinery which divides responsibility for misdeeds in such a way that no one feels them to be contrary to nature.

Some make the laws, others execute them; some train

men by discipline to automatic obedience; and these last, in their turn, become the instruments of coercion, and slay their kind without knowing why or to what end. But let a man disentangle himself for a moment from this compli-cated network, and he will readily see that coercion is con-trary to his nature. Let us abstain from affirming that organized violence, of which we make use to our own profit, is a divine, immutable law, and we shall see clearly which is most in harmony with human nature,—the doc-trine of violence or the doctrine of Jesus.

What is the law of nature? Is it to know that my security and that of my family, all my amusements and pleasures, are purchased at the expense of misery, deprivation, and suffering to thousands of human beings—by the terror of the gallows; by the misfortune of thousands stifling within prison walls; by the fear inspired by millions of soldiers and guardians of civilization, torn from their homes and besot-ted by discipline, to protect our pleasures with loaded re-volvers against the possible interference of the famishing? Is it to purchase every fragment of bread that I put in my mouth and the mouths of my children by the numberless privations that are necessary to procure my abundance? Or is it to be certain that my piece of bread only belongs to me when I know that every one else has a share, and that no one starves while I eat?

It is only necessary to understand that, thanks to our so-cial organization, each one of our pleasures, every minute of our cherished tranquillity, is obtained by the sufferings and privations of thousands of our fellows—it is only nec-essary to understand this, to know what is conformable to human nature; not to our animal nature alone, but the ani-mal and spiritual nature which constitutes man. When we once understand the doctrine of Jesus in all its bearings, with all its consequences, we shall be convinced that his doctrine is not contrary to human nature; but that its sole object is to supplant the chimerical law of the struggle against evil by violence—itself the law contrary to human nature and productive of so many evils.

Do you say that the doctrine of Jesus, *"Resist not evil,"* is vain? What, then, are we to think of the lives of those who are not filled with love and compassion for their kind,—of those who make ready for their fellow-men punishment at the stake, by the knout, the wheel, the rack, chains, compulsory labor, the gibbet, dungeons, prisons for women and children, the hecatombs of war, or bring about periodical revolutions; of those who carry these horrors into execution; of those who benefit by these calamities or prepare reprisals,—are not such lives vain?

We need only understand the doctrine of Jesus, to be convinced that existence,—not the reasonable existence which gives happiness to humanity, but the existence men have organized to their own hurt,—that such an existence is a vanity, the most savage and horrible of vanities, a veritable delirium of folly, to which, once reclaimed, we do not again return.

God descended to earth, became incarnate to redeem Adam's sin, and (so we were taught to believe) said many mysterious and mystical things which are difficult to understand, which it is not possible to understand except by the aid of faith and grace—and suddenly the words of God are found to be simple, clear, and reasonable! God said, Do no evil, and evil will cease to exist. Was the revelation from God really so simple—nothing but that? It would seem that every one might understand it, it is so simple!

The prophet Elijah, a fugitive from men, took refuge in a cave, and was told that God would appear to him. There came a great wind that devastated the forest; Elijah thought that the Lord had come, but the Lord was not in the wind.

After the wind came the thunder and the lightning, but God was not there. Then came the earthquake: the earth belched forth fire, the rocks were shattered, the mountain was rent to its foundations; Elijah looked for the Lord, but the Lord was not in the earthquake. Then, in the calm that followed, a gentle breeze came to the prophet, bearing the freshness of the fields; and Elijah knew that God was there. It is a magnificent illustration of the words, *"Resist not evil."*

They are very simple, these words; but they are, nevertheless, the expression of a law divine and human. If there has been in history a progressive movement for the suppression of evil, it is due to the men who understood the doctrine of Jesus—who endured evil, and resisted not evil by violence. The advance of humanity towards righteousness is due, not to the tyrants, but to the martyrs. As fire cannot extinguish fire, so evil cannot suppress evil. Good alone, confronting evil and resisting its contagion, can overcome evil. And in the inner world of the human soul, the law is as absolute as was even the law of Galileo, more absolute, more clear, more immutable. Men may turn aside from it, they may hide its truth from others; but the progress of humanity towards righteousness can only be attained in this way. Every step must be guided by the command, *"Resist not evil."* A disciple of Jesus may say now, with greater assurance than did Galileo, in spite of misfortunes and threats: "And yet it is not violence, but good, that overcomes evil." If the progress is slow, it is because the doctrine of Jesus (which, through its clearness, simplicity, and wisdom, appeals so inevitably to human nature), because the doctrine of Jesus has been cunningly concealed from the majority of mankind under an entirely different doctrine falsely called by his name.

V

THE true meaning of the doctrine of Jesus was revealed to me; everything confirmed its truth. But for a long time I could not accustom myself to the strange fact, that after the eighteen centuries during which the law of Jesus had been professed by millions of human beings, after the eighteen centuries during which thousands of men had consecrated their lives to the study of this law, I had discovered it for myself anew. But strange as it seemed, so it was. Jesus' law, *"Resist not evil,"* was to me wholly new, something of which I had never had any conception before. I asked myself how this could be; I must certainly have had a false idea of the doctrine of Jesus to cause such a misunderstanding. And a false idea of it I unquestionably had. When I began to read the Gospel, I was not in the condition of one who, having heard nothing of the doctrine of Jesus, becomes acquainted with it for the first time; on the contrary, I had a preconceived theory as to the manner in which I ought to understand it. Jesus did not appeal to me as a prophet revealing the divine law, but as one who continued and amplified the absolute divine law which I already knew; for I had very definite and complex notions about God, the creator of the world and of man, and about the commandments of God given to men through the instrumentality of Moses.

When I came to the words, *"Ye have heard that it hath been said, An eye for an eye, and a tooth for a tooth: But I say unto you, That ye resist not evil,"*—the words, *"An eye for an eye, and a tooth for a tooth,"* expressed the law given by God to Moses;

the words, *"But I say unto you, That ye resist not evil,"* expressed the new law, which was a negation of the first. If I
had seen Jesus' words, simply, in their true sense, and not
as a part of the theological theory that I had imbibed at my
mother's breast, I should have understood immediately
that Jesus abrogated the old law, and substituted for it a
new law. But I had been taught that Jesus did not abrogate
the law of Moses, that, on the contrary, he confirmed it to
the slightest iota, and that he made it more complete. Verses
17–20 of the fifth chapter of Matthew always impressed me,
when I read the Gospel, by their obscurity, and they
plunged me into doubt. I knew the Old Testament, particularly the last books of Moses, very thoroughly, and recalling
certain passages in which minute doctrines, often absurd
and even cruel in their purport, are preceded by the words,
"And the Lord said unto Moses," it seemed to me very singular that Jesus should confirm all these injunctions; I could
not understand why he did so. But I allowed the question to
pass without solution, and accepted with confidence the explanations inculcated in my infancy,—that the two laws
were equally inspired by the Holy Spirit, that they were in
perfect accord, and that Jesus confirmed the law of Moses
while completing and amplifying it. I did not concern myself with accounting for the process of this amplification,
with the solution of the contradictions apparent throughout
the whole Gospel, in verses 17–20 of the fifth chapter, in the
words, *"But I say unto you."*

Now that I understood the clear and simple meaning of
the doctrine of Jesus, I saw clearly that the two laws are directly opposed to one another; that they can never be har-
monized; that, instead of supplementing one by the other,
we must inevitably choose between the two; and that the
received explanation of the verses, Matthew v. 17–20, which
had impressed me by their obscurity, must be incorrect.

When I now came to read once more the verses that had before impressed me as obscure, I was astonished at the clear and simple meaning which was suddenly revealed to me. This meaning was revealed, not by any combination and transposition, but solely by rejecting the factitious explanations with which the words had been encumbered. According to Matthew, Jesus said (v. 17–18):—

"Think not that I am come to destroy the law, or the prophets (the doctrine of the prophets): *I am not come to destroy, but to fulfil. For verily I say unto you, Till heaven and earth pass, one jot or one tittle shall in no wise pass from the law, till all be fulfilled."*

And in verse 20 he added:—

"For I say unto you, That except your righteousness shall exceed the righteousness of the scribes and Pharisees, ye shall in no case enter into the kingdom of heaven."

I am not come (Jesus said) to destroy the eternal law of whose fulfilment your books of prophecy foretell. I am come to teach you the fulfilment of the eternal law; not of the law that your scribes and pharisees call the divine law, but of that eternal law which is more immutable than the earth and the heavens.

I have expressed the idea in other words in order to detach the thoughts of my readers from the traditional false interpretation. If this false interpretation had never existed, the idea expressed in the verses could not be rendered in a better or more definite manner.

The view that Jesus did not abrogate the old law arises from the arbitrary conclusion that "law" in this passage signifies the written law instead of the law eternal, the reference to the iota—jot and tittle—perhaps furnishing the grounds for such an opinion. But if Jesus had been speaking of the written law, he would have used the expression "the law and the prophets," which he always employed in speaking of the written law; here, however, he uses a different expression,—"the law *or* the prophets." If Jesus had meant the written law, he would have used the expression, "the law and the prophets," in the verses that follow and that continue the thought; but he says, briefly, "the law." Moreover, according to Luke, Jesus made use of the same phraseology, and the context renders the meaning inevitable. According to Luke, Jesus said to the Pharisees, who assumed the justice of their written law:—

"Ye are they which justify yourselves before men; but God knoweth your hearts: for that which is highly esteemed among men is abomination in the sight of God. The law and the prophets were until John: since that time the kingdom of God is preached, and every man presseth into it. And it is easier for heaven and earth to pass, than one tittle of the law to fail." (Luke xvi. 15–17.)

In the words, *"The law and the prophets were until John,"* Jesus abrogated the written law; in the words, *"And it is easier for heaven and earth to pass, than one tittle of* the law *to fail,"* Jesus confirmed the law eternal. In the first passage cited he said, "the law *and* the prophets," that is, the written law; in the second he said "the law" simply, therefore the law eternal. It is clear, then, that the eternal law is opposed to the written law,[1] exactly as in the context of Matthew where the eternal law is defined by the phrase, "the law *or* the prophets."

The history of the variants of the text of these verses is

---

[1]More than this, as if to do away with all doubt about the law to which he referred, Jesus cites immediately, in connection with this passage, the most decisive instance of the negation of the law of Moses by the eternal law, the law of which not the smallest jot is to fail: *"Whosoever putteth away his wife, and marrieth another, committeth adultery."* (Luke xvi. 18.) That is, according to the written law divorce is permissible; according to the eternal law it is forbidden.

quite worthy of notice. The majority of texts have simply "the law," without the addition, "and the prophets," thus avoiding a false interpretation in the sense of the written law. In other texts, notably that of Tischendorf, and in the canonical versions, we find the word "prophets" used, not with the conjunction "and," but with the conjunction "or,"—"the law *or* the prophets,"—which also excludes any question of the written law, and indicates, as the proper signification, the law eternal. In several other versions, not countenanced by the Church, we find the word "prophets" used with the conjunction "and," not with "or"; and in these versions every repetition of the words "the law" is followed by the phrase, "and the prophets," which would indicate that Jesus spoke only of the written law.

The history of the commentaries on the passage in question coincides with that of the variants. The only clear meaning is that authorized by Luke,—that Jesus spoke of the eternal law. But among the copyists of the Gospel were some who desired that the written law of Moses should continue to be regarded as obligatory. They therefore added to the words "the law" the phrase "and the prophets," and thereby changed the interpretation of the text.

Other Christians, not recognizing to the same degree the authority of the books of Moses, suppressed the added phrase, and replaced the particle καί, "and," with ἤ, "or"; and with this substitution the passage was admitted to the canon. Nevertheless, in spite of the unequivocal clearness of the text as thus written, the commentators perpetuated the interpretation supported by the phrase which had been rejected in the canon. The passage evoked innumerable comments, which stray from the true signification in proportion to the lack, on the part of the commentators, of fidelity to the simple and obvious meaning of Jesus' doctrine.

Most of them recognize the reading rejected by the canonical text.

To be absolutely convinced that Jesus spoke only of the eternal law, we need only examine the true meaning of the word which has given rise to so many false interpretations. The word "law" (in Greek νόμος, in Hebrew תּוֹרָה, *torah*) has in all languages two principal meanings: one, law in the abstract sense, independent of formulæ; the other, the written statutes which men generally recognize as law. In the Greek of Paul's Epistles the distinction is indicated by the use of the article. Without the article Paul uses νόμος the most frequently in the sense of the divine eternal law. By the ancient Hebrews, as in books of Isaiah and the other prophets, תּוֹרָה, *torah*, is always used in the sense of an eternal revelation, a divine intuition. It was not till the time of Esdras, and later in the Talmud, that "Torah" was used in the same sense in which we use the word "Bible"—with this difference, that while we have words to distinguish between the Bible and the divine law, the Jews employed the same word to express both meanings.

And so Jesus sometimes speaks of law as the divine law (of Isaiah and the other prophets), in which case he confirms it; and sometimes in the sense of the written law of the Pentateuch, in which case he rejects it. To distinguish the difference, he always, in speaking of the written law, adds, "and the prophets," or prefixes the word "your,"—"your law."

When he says: *"Therefore all things whatsoever ye would that men should do to you, do ye even so to them: for this is the law and the prophets"* (Matt. vii. 12), he speaks of the written law. The entire written law, he says, may be reduced to this expression of the eternal law, and by these words he abrogated the written law. When he says, *"The law and the prophets were until John"* (Luke xvi. 16), he speaks of the written law, and abrogates it. When he says, *"Did not Moses give you the law, and yet none of you keepeth the law"* (John vii. 19), *"It is also written in your law"* (John viii. 17), *"that the word might be fulfilled that is written in their law"* (John xv. 25), he speaks of the written law, the law whose authority he denied, the law that condemned him to death: *"The Jews answered him, We have a law, and by our law he ought to die"* (John xix. 7). It is plain that this Jewish law, which authorized condemnation to death, was not the law of Jesus. But when Jesus says, "I am not come to destroy the law, but to teach you the fulfilment of the law; for nothing of this law shall be changed, but all shall be fulfilled," then he speaks, not of the written law, but of the divine and eternal law.

Admit that all this is merely formal proof; admit that I have carefully combined contexts and variants, and excluded everything contrary to my theory; admit that the commentators of the Church are clear and convincing, that, in fact, Jesus did not abrogate the law of Moses, but upheld it—admit this: then the question is, what were the teachings of Jesus?

According to the Church, he taught that he was the second person of the Trinity, the Son of God, and that he came into the world to atone by his death for Adam's sin. Those, however, who have read the Gospels know that Jesus taught nothing of the sort, or at least spoke but very vaguely on these topics. The passages in which Jesus affirms that he is the second person of the Trinity, and that he was to atone for the sins of humanity, form a very inconsiderable and very obscure portion of the Gospels. In what, then, does the rest of Jesus' doctrine consist? It is impossible to deny, for all Christians have recognized the fact, that the doctrine of Jesus aims summarily to regulate the lives of men, to teach them how they ought to live with regard to one another. But to realize that Jesus taught men a new way of life, we must have some idea of the condition of the people to whom his teachings were addressed.

When we examine into the social development of the Russians, the English, the Chinese, the Indians, or even the races of insular savages, we find that each people invariably has certain practical rules or laws which govern its existence; consequently, if any one would inculcate a new law, he must at the same time abolish the old; in any race or nation this would be inevitable. Laws that we are accustomed to regard as almost sacred would assuredly be abrogated; with us, perhaps, it might happen that a reformer who taught a new law would abolish only our civil laws, the official code, our administrative customs, without touching what we consider as our divine laws, although it is difficult to believe that such could be the case. But with the Jewish people, who had but one law, and that recognized as divine,—a law which enveloped life to its minutest details,— what could a reformer accomplish if he declared in advance that the existing law was inviolable?

Admit that this argument is not conclusive, and try to interpret the words of Jesus as an affirmation of the entire Mosaic law; in that case, who were the Pharisees, the scribes, the doctors of the law denounced by Jesus during the whole of his ministry? Who were they that rejected the doctrine of Jesus and, their High Priests at their head, crucified him? If Jesus approved the law of Moses, where were the faithful followers of that law, who practised it sincerely, and must thereby have obtained Jesus' approval? Is it possible that there was not one such? The Pharisees, we are told, constituted a sect; where, then, were the righteous?

In the Gospel of John the enemies of Jesus are spoken of directly as "the Jews." They are opposed to the doctrine of Jesus; they are hostile because they are Jews. But it is not only the Pharisees and the Sadducees who figure in the

Gospels as the enemies of Jesus: we also find mention of the doctors of the law, the guardians of the law of Moses, the scribes, the interpreters of the law, the ancients, those who are always considered as representatives of the people's wisdom. Jesus said, *"I am not come to call the righteous, but sinners to repentance,"* to change their way of life ($\mu\varepsilon\tau\acute{a}\nu o\iota a$). But where were the righteous? Was Nicodemus the only one? He is represented as a good, but misguided man.

We are so habituated to the singular opinion that Jesus was crucified by the Pharisees and a number of Jewish shopkeepers, that we never think to ask, Where were the true Jews, the good Jews, the Jews that practised the law? When we have once propounded this query, everything becomes perfectly clear. Jesus, whether he was God or man, brought his doctrine to a people possessing rules, called the divine law, governing their whole existence. How could Jesus avoid denouncing that law?

Every prophet, every founder of a religion, inevitably meets, in revealing the divine law to men, with institutions which are regarded as upheld by the laws of God. He cannot, therefore, avoid a double use of the word "law," which expresses what his hearers wrongfully consider the law of God ("your law"), and the law he has come to proclaim, the true law, the divine and eternal law. A reformer not only cannot avoid the use of the word in this manner; often he does not wish to avoid it, but purposely confounds the two ideas, thus indicating that, in the law confessed by those whom he would convert, there are still some eternal truths. Every reformer takes these truths, so well known to his hearers, as the basis of his teaching. This is precisely what Jesus did in addressing the Jews, by whom the two laws were vaguely grouped together as "Torah." Jesus recognized that the Mosaic law, and still more the prophetical books, especially the writings of Isaiah, whose words he constantly quotes,—Jesus recognized that these contained divine and eternal truths in harmony with the eternal law, and these he takes as the basis of his own doctrine. This method was many times referred to by Jesus; thus he said, *"What is written in the law? how readest thou?"* (Luke x. 26). That is, one may find eternal truth in the law, if one reads it aright. And more than once he affirms that the commandments of the Mosaic law, to love the Lord and one's neighbor, are also commandments of the eternal law. At the conclusion of the parables by which Jesus explained the meaning of his doctrine to his disciples, he pronounced words that have a bearing upon all that precedes:—

"Therefore every scribe which is instructed unto the kingdom of heaven (the truth) *is like unto a man that is a householder, which bringeth forth out of his treasure* (without distinction) *things new and old."* (Matt. xiii. 52.)

The Church understands these words, as they were understood by Irenæus; but at the same time, in defiance of the true signification, it arbitrarily attributes to them the meaning that everything old is sacred. The manifest meaning is this: He who seeks for the good, takes not only the new, but also the old; and because a thing is old, he does not therefore reject it. By these words Jesus meant that he did not deny what was eternal in the old law. But when they spoke to him of the whole law, or of the formalities exacted by the old law, his reply was that new wine should not be put into old bottles. Jesus could not affirm the whole law; neither could he deny the entire teachings of the law and the prophets,—the law which says, *"love thy neighbor as thyself,"* the prophets whose words often served to express his own thoughts. And yet, in place of this clear and simple explanation of Jesus' words, we are offered a vague interpretation which introduces needless contradictions, which

reduces the doctrine of Jesus to nothingness, and which re-
establishes the doctrine of Moses in all its savage cruelty.

Commentators of the Church, particularly those who
have written since the fifth century, tell us that Jesus did not
abolish the written law; that, on the contrary, he affirmed it.
But in what way? How is it possible that the law of Jesus
should harmonize with the law of Moses? To these inquiries
we get no response. The commentators all make use of a
verbal juggle to the effect that Jesus fulfilled the law of
Moses, and that the sayings of the prophets were fulfilled in
his person; that Jesus fulfilled the law as our mediator by
our faith in him. And the essential question for every believer—How to harmonize two conflicting laws, each de-
signed to regulate the lives of men?—is left without the
slightest attempt at explanation. Thus the contradiction between the verse where it is said that Jesus did not come to
destroy the law, but to fulfil the law, and Jesus' saying, *"Ye
have heard that it hath been said, An eye for an eye . . . But I say
unto you,"*—the contradiction between the doctrine of Jesus
and the very spirit of the Mosaic doctrine,—is left without
any mitigation.

Let those who are interested in the question look through
the Church commentaries touching this passage from the
time of Chrysostom to our day. After a perusal of the volu-
minous explanations offered, they will be convinced not
only of the complete absence of any solution for the contradiction, but of the presence of a new, factitious contradiction arising in its place. Let us see what Chrysostom says in
reply to those who reject the law of Moses:—

"He made this law, not that we might strike out one another's eyes, but that fear of suffering by others might restrain us from doing any such thing to them. As therefore
He threatened the Ninevites with overthrow, not that He
might destroy them (for had that been His will, He ought to

have been silent), but that He might by fear make them better, and so quiet His wrath: so also hath He appointed a punishment for those who wantonly assail the eyes of others, that if good principle dispose them not to refrain from such cruelty, fear may restrain them from injuring their neighbors' sight.

"And if this be cruelty, it is cruelty also for the murderer to be restrained, and the adulterer checked. But these are the sayings of senseless men, and of those that are mad to the extreme of madness. For I, so far from saying that this comes of cruelty, should say that the contrary to this would be unlawful, according to men's reckoning. And whereas thou sayest, 'Because He commanded to pluck out *an eye for an eye*, therefore He is cruel'; I say that if He had not given this commandment, then He would have seemed, in the judgment of most men, to be that which thou sayest He is."

Chrysostom clearly recognized the law, *An eye for an eye*, as divine, and the contrary of that law, that is, the doctrine of Jesus, *Resist not evil*, as an iniquity. "For let us suppose," says Chrysostom further:—

"For let us suppose that this law had been altogether done away, and that no one feared the punishment ensuing thereupon, but that license had been given to all the wicked to follow their own dispositions in all security, to adulterers, and to murderers, to perjured persons, and to parricides; would not all things have been turned upside down? would not cities, market-places and houses, sea and land, and the whole world have been filled with unnumbered pollutions and murders? Every one sees it. For if, when there are laws, and fear, and threatening, our evil dispositions are hardly checked; were even this security taken away, what is there to prevent men's choosing vice? and what degree of mischief would not then come revelling upon the whole of human life?

"The rather, since cruelty lies not only in allowing the bad to do what they will, but in another thing too quite as much,—to overlook, and leave uncared for, him who hath done no wrong, but who is without cause or reason suffering ill. For tell me; were any one to gather together wicked men from all quarters, and arm them with swords, and bid them go about the whole city, and massacre all that came in their way, could there be anything more like a wild beast than he? And what if some others should bind, and confine with the utmost strictness, those whom that man had armed, and should snatch from those lawless hands them who were on the point of being butchered; could anything be greater humanity than this?"

Chrysostom does not say what would be the estimate of these others in the opinion of the wicked. And what if these others were themselves wicked and cast the innocent into prison? Chrysostom continues:—

"Now then, I bid thee transfer these examples to the Law likewise; for He that commands to pluck out *an eye for an eye* hath laid the fear as a kind of strong chain upon the souls of the bad, and so resembles him who detains those assassins in prison; whereas he who appoints no punishment for them, doth all but arm them by such security, and acts the part of that other, who was putting the swords in their hands, and letting them loose over the whole city." ("Homilies on the Gospel of St. Matthew," xvi.)

If Chrysostom had understood the law of Jesus, he would have said, Who is it that strikes out another's eyes? who is it that casts men into prison? If God, who made the law, does this, then there is no contradiction; but it is men who carry out the decrees, and the Son of God has said to men that they must abstain from violence. God commanded to strike out, and the Son of God commanded not to strike out. We must accept one commandment or the

other; and Chrysostom, like all the rest of the Church, accepted the commandment of Moses and denied that of the
Christ, whose doctrine he nevertheless claims to believe.

Jesus abolished the Mosaic law, and gave his own law in
its place. To one who really believes in Jesus there is not the
slightest contradiction; such an one will pay no attention to
the law of Moses, but will practise the law of Jesus, which
he believes. To one who believes in the law of Moses there is
no contradiction. The Jews looked upon the words of Jesus
as foolishness, and believed in the law of Moses. The contradiction is only for those who would follow the law of
Moses under the cover of the law of Jesus—for those whom
Jesus denounced as hypocrites, as a generation of vipers.

Instead of recognizing as divine truth the one or the other
of the two laws, the law of Moses or that of Jesus, we recognize the divine quality of both. But when the question
comes with regard to the acts of every-day life, we reject the
law of Jesus and follow that of Moses. And this false interpretation, when we realize its importance, reveals the
source of that terrible drama which records the struggle between evil and good, between darkness and light.

To the Jewish people, trained to the innumerable formal
regulations instituted by the Levites in the rubric of divine
laws, each preceded by the words, "And the Lord said unto
Moses"—to the Jewish people Jesus appeared. He found
everything, to the minutest detail, prescribed by rule; not
only the relation of man with God, but his sacrifices, his
feasts, his fasts, his social, civil, and family duties, the details of personal habits, circumcision, the purification of the
body, of domestic utensils, of clothing—all these regulated
by laws recognized as commandments of God, and therefore as divine.

Excluding the question of Jesus' divine mission, what
could any prophet or reformer do who wished to establish

his own doctrines among a people so enveloped in formalism—what but abolish the law by which all these details were regulated? Jesus selected from what men considered as the law of God the portions which were really divine; he took what served his purpose, rejected the rest, and upon this foundation established the eternal law. It was not necessary to abolish all, but inevitable to abrogate much that was looked upon as obligatory. This Jesus did, and was accused of destroying the divine law; for this he was condemned and put to death. But his doctrine was cherished by his disciples, traversed the centuries, and is transmitted to other peoples. Under these conditions it is again hidden beneath heterogeneous dogmas, obscure comments, and factitious explanations. Pitiable human sophisms replace the divine revelation. For the formula, "And the Lord said unto Moses," we substitute "Thus saith the Holy Spirit." And again formalism hides the truth. Most astounding of all, the doctrine of Jesus is amalgamated with the written law, whose authority he was forced to deny. This *Torah,* this written law, is declared to have been inspired by the Holy Spirit, the spirit of truth; and thus Jesus is taken in the snare of his own revelation—his doctrine is reduced to nothingness.

This is why, after eighteen hundred years, it so singularly happened that I discovered the meaning of the doctrine of Jesus as some new thing. But no; I did not discover it; I did simply what all must do who seek after God and His law; I sought for the eternal law amid the incongruous elements that men call by that name.

VI

THE doctrine of Jesus is to bring the kingdom of God upon earth. The practice of this doctrine is not difficult; and not only so, its practice is a natural expression of the belief of all who recognize its truth. The doctrine of Jesus offers the only possible chance of salvation for those who would escape the perdition that threatens the personal life. The fulfilment of this doctrine not only will deliver men from the privations and sufferings of this life, but will put an end to nine-tenths of the suffering endured in behalf of the doctrine of the world.

When I understood this I asked myself why I had never practised a doctrine which would give me so much happiness and peace and joy; why, on the other hand, I always had practised an entirely different doctrine, and thereby made myself wretched? Why? The reply was a simple one. Because I never had known the truth. The truth had been concealed from me.

When the doctrine of Jesus was first revealed to me, I did not believe that the discovery would lead me to reject the doctrine of the Church. I dreaded this separation, and in the course of my studies I did not attempt to search out the errors in the doctrine of the Church. I sought, rather, to close my eyes to propositions that seemed to be obscure and strange, provided they were not in evident contradiction with what I regarded as the substance of the Christian doctrine.

But the further I advanced in the study of the Gospels,

and the more clearly the doctrine of Jesus was revealed to me, the more inevitable the choice became. I must either accept the doctrine of Jesus, a reasonable and simple doctrine in accordance with my conscience and my hope of salvation; or I must accept an entirely different doctrine, a doctrine in opposition to reason and conscience and that offered me nothing except the certainty of my own perdition and that of others. I was therefore forced to reject, one after another, the dogmas of the Church. This I did against my will, struggling with the desire to mitigate as much as possible my disagreement with the Church, that I might not be obliged to separate from the Church, and thereby deprive myself of communion with fellow-believers, the greatest happiness that religion can bestow. But when I had completed my task, I saw that in spite of all my efforts to maintain a connecting link with the Church, the separation was complete. I knew before that the bond of union, if it existed at all, must be a very slight one, but I was soon convinced that it did not exist at all.

My son came to me one day, after I had completed my examination of the Gospels, and told me of a discussion that was going on between two domestics (uneducated persons who scarcely knew how to read) concerning a passage in some religious book which maintained that it was not a sin to put criminals to death, or to kill enemies in war. I could not believe that an assertion of this sort could be printed in any book, and I asked to see it. The volume bore the title of "*A Book of Selected Prayers;* third edition; eighth ten thousand; Moscow: 1879." On page 163 of this book I read:—

"What is the sixth commandment of God?

"Thou shalt not kill.

"What does God forbid by this commandment?

"He forbids us to kill, to take the life of any man.

"Is it a sin to punish a criminal with death according to the law, or to kill an enemy in war?

"No; that is not a sin. We take the life of the criminal to put an end to the wrong that he commits; we slay an enemy in war, because in war we fight for our sovereign and our native land."

And in this manner was enjoined the abrogation of the law of God! I could scarcely believe that I had read aright.

My opinion was asked with regard to the subject at issue. To the one who maintained that the instruction given by the book was true, I said that the explanation was not correct.

"Why, then, do they print untrue explanations contrary to the law?" was his question, to which I could say nothing in reply.

I kept the volume and looked over its contents. The book contained thirty-one prayers with instructions concerning genuflexions and the joining of the fingers; an explanation of the *Credo;* a citation from the fifth chapter of Matthew without any explanation whatever, but headed, "Commands for those who would possess the Beatitudes"; the ten commandments accompanied by comments that rendered most of them void; and hymns for every saint's day.

As I have said, I not only had sought to avoid censure of the religion of the Church; I had done my best to see only its most favorable side; and knowing its academic literature from beginning to end, I had paid no attention whatever to its popular literature. This book of devotion, spread broadcast in an enormous number of copies, awakening doubts in the minds of the most unlearned people, set me to thinking. The contents of the book seemed to me so entirely pagan, so wholly out of accord with Christianity, that I could not believe it to be the deliberate purpose of the Church to propagate such a doctrine. To verify my belief, I bought and read all the books published by the synod with its "benediction" *(blagoslovnia)*, containing brief expositions of the religion of the Church for the use of children and the common people.

Their contents were to me almost entirely new, for at the time when I received my early religious instruction, they had not yet appeared. As far as I could remember there were no commandments with regard to the beatitudes, and there was no doctrine which taught that it was not a sin to kill. No such teachings appeared in the old catechisms; they were not to be found in the catechism of Peter Mogilas, or in that of Beliokof, or the abridged Catholic catechisms. The innovation was introduced by the metropolitan Philaret, who prepared a catechism with proper regard for the sus- ceptibilities of the military class, and from this catechism the *Book of Selected Prayers* was compiled. Philaret's work is entitled, *The Christian Catechism of the Orthodox Church, for the Use of all Orthodox Christians,* and is published, "by order of his Imperial Majesty."[1]

The book is divided into three parts, "Concerning Faith," "Concerning Hope," and "Concerning Love." The first part contains the analysis of the symbol of faith as given by the Council of Nice. The second part is made up of an exposi- tion of the *Pater Noster,* and the first eight verses of the fifth chapter of Matthew, which serve as an introduction to the Sermon on the Mount, and are called (I know not why) "Commands for those who would possess the Beatitudes." These first two parts treat of the dogmas of the Church, prayers, and the sacraments, but they contain no rules with regard to the conduct of life. The third part, "Concerning

---

[1]This book has been in use in all the schools and churches of Russia since 1839.—TR.

Love," contains an exposition of Christian duties, based not on the commandments of Jesus, but upon the ten commandments of Moses. This exposition of the commandments of Moses seems to have been made for the especial purpose of teaching men not to obey them. Each commandment is followed by a reservation which completely destroys its force. With regard to the first commandment, which enjoins the worship of God alone, the catechism inculcates the worship of saints and angels, to say nothing of the Mother of God and the three persons of the Trinity ("Special Catechism," pp. 107, 108). With regard to the second commandment, against the worship of idols, the catechism enjoins the worship of images (p. 108). With regard to the third commandment, the catechism enjoins the taking of oaths as the principal token of legitimate authority (p. 111). With regard to the fourth commandment, concerning the observance of the Sabbath, the catechism inculcates the observance of Sunday, of the thirteen principal feasts, of a number of feasts of less importance, the observance of Lent, and of fasts on Wednesdays and Fridays (pp. 112–115). With regard to the fifth commandment, *"Honor thy father and thy mother,"* the catechism prescribes honor to the sovereign, the country, spiritual fathers, all persons in authority, and of these last gives an enumeration in three pages, including college authorities, civil, judicial, and military authorities, and owners of serfs, with instructions as to the manner of honoring each of these classes (pp. 116–119). My citations are taken from the sixty-fourth edition of the catechism, dated 1880. Twenty years have passed since the abolition of serfdom, and no one has taken the trouble to strike out the phrase which, in connection with the commandment of God to honor parents, was introduced into the catechism to sustain and justify slavery.

With regard to the sixth commandment, *"Thou shalt not kill,"* the instructions of the catechism are from the first in favor of murder.

"Question.—What does the sixth commandment forbid?

"Answer.—It forbids manslaughter, to take the life of one's neighbor in any manner whatever.

"Question.—Is all manslaughter a transgression of the law?

"Answer.—Manslaughter is not a transgression of the law when life is taken in pursuance of its mandate. For example:

"1st. When a criminal condemned in justice is punished by death.

"2d. When we kill *in war* for the sovereign and our country."

The italics are in the original. Further on we read:—

"Question.—With regard to manslaughter, when is the law transgressed?

"Answer.—When any one conceals a murderer or sets him at liberty" *(sic).*

All this is printed in hundreds of thousands of copies, and under the name of Christian doctrine is taught by compulsion to every Russian, who is obliged to receive it under penalty of castigation. This is taught to all the Russian people. It is taught to the innocent children,—to the children whom Jesus commanded to be brought to him as belonging to the kingdom of God; to the children whom we must resemble, in ignorance of false doctrines, to enter into the kingdom of God; to the children whom Jesus tried to protect in proclaiming woe on him who should cause one of the little ones to stumble! And the little children are obliged to learn all this, and are told that it is the only and sacred law of God. These are not proclamations sent out clandestinely, whose authors are punished with penal servitude;

they are proclamations which inflict the punishment of penal servitude upon all those who do not agree with the doctrines they inculcate.

As I write these lines, I experience a feeling of insecurity, simply because I have allowed myself to say that men cannot render void the fundamental law of God inscribed in all the codes and in all hearts, by such words as these:—

"Manslaughter is not a transgression of the law when life is taken in pursuance of its mandate. . . . when we kill in war for our sovereign and our country."

I tremble because I have allowed myself to say that such things should not be taught to children.

It was against such teachings as these that Jesus warned men when he said:—

"Look, therefore, whether the light that is in thee be not darkness." (Luke xi. 35.)

The light that is in us has become darkness; and the darkness of our lives is full of terror.

"Woe unto you, scribes and Pharisees, hypocrites! because ye shut the kingdom of heaven against men: for ye enter not in yourselves, neither suffer ye them that are entering in to enter. Woe unto you, scribes and Pharisees, hypocrites! for ye devour widows' houses, even while for a pretence ye make long prayers: therefore ye shall receive greater condemnation. Woe unto you, scribes and Pharisees, hypocrites! for ye compass sea and land to make one proselyte; and when he is become so, ye make him twofold more a son of hell than yourselves. Woe unto you, ye blind guides. . . .

"Woe unto you, scribes and Pharisees, hypocrites! for ye build the sepulchres of the prophets, and garnish the tombs of the righteous, and say, If we had been in the days of our fathers, we should not have been partakers with them in the blood of the prophets. Wherefore ye witness to yourselves, that ye are sons of them that slew the prophets. Fill ye up, then, the measure of your fathers. . . .

I send unto you prophets, and wise men, and scribes: some of them shall ye kill and crucify; and some of them shall ye scourge in your synagogues, and persecute from city to city: that upon you may come all the righteous blood shed on the earth, from the blood of Abel. . . .

"*Every sin and blasphemy shall be forgiven unto men; but the blasphemy against the Spirit shall not be forgiven.*"

Of a truth we might say that all this was written but yesterday, not against men who no longer compass sea and land to blaspheme against the Spirit, or to convert men to a religion that renders its proselytes worse than they were before, but against men who deliberately force people to embrace their religion, and persecute and bring to death all the prophets and the righteous who seek to reveal their falsehoods to mankind. I became convinced that the doctrine of the Church, although bearing the name of "Christian," is one with the darkness against which Jesus struggled, and against which he commanded his disciples to strive.

The doctrine of Jesus, like all religious doctrines, is regarded in two ways,—first, as a moral and ethical system which teaches men how they should live as individuals, and in relation to each other; second, as a metaphysical theory which explains why men should live in a given manner and not otherwise. One necessitates the other. Man should live in this manner because such is his destiny; or, man's destiny is this way, and consequently he should follow it. These two methods of doctrinal expression are common to all the religions of the world, to the religion of the Brahmins, to that of Confucius, to that of Buddha, to that of Moses, and to that of the Christ. But, with regard to the doctrine of Jesus, as with regard to all other doctrines, men wander from its precepts, and they always find some one to justify their deviations. Those who, as Jesus said, sit in

Moses' seat, explain the metaphysical theory in such a way that the ethical prescriptions of the doctrine cease to be regarded as obligatory, and are replaced by external forms of worship, by ceremonial. This is a condition common to all religions, but, to me, it seems that it never has been manifested with so much pomp as in connection with Christianity,—and for two reasons: first, because the doctrine of Jesus is the most elevated of all doctrines (the most elevated because the metaphysical and ethical portions are so closely united that one cannot be separated from the other without destroying the vitality of the whole); second, because the doctrine of Jesus is in itself a protest against all forms, a negation not only of Jewish ceremonial, but of all exterior rites of worship. Therefore, the arbitrary separation of the metaphysical and ethical aspects of Christianity entirely disfigures the doctrine, and deprives it of every sort of meaning. The separation began with the preaching of Paul, who knew but imperfectly the ethical doctrine set forth in the Gospel of Matthew, and who preached a metaphysico-cabalistic theory entirely foreign to the doctrine of Jesus; and this theory was perfected under Constantine, when the existing pagan social organization was proclaimed Christian simply by covering it with the mantle of Christianity. After Constantine, that arch-pagan, whom the Church in spite of all his crimes and vices admits to the category of the saints, after Constantine began the domination of the councils, and the centre of gravity of Christianity was permanently displaced till only the metaphysical portion was left in view. And this metaphysical theory with its accompanying ceremonial deviated more and more from its true and primitive meaning, until it has reached its present stage of development, as a doctrine which explains the mysteries of a celestial life beyond the comprehension of human reason, and, with all its complicated formulas, gives no religious guidance whatever with regard to the regulation of this earthly life.

All religions, with the exception of the religion of the Christian Church, demand from their adherents aside from forms and ceremonies, the practice of certain actions called good, and abstinence from certain actions that are called bad. The Jewish religion prescribed circumcision, the observance of the Sabbath, the giving of alms, the feast of the Passover. Mohammedanism prescribes circumcision, prayer five times a day, the giving of tithes to the poor, pilgrimage to the tomb of the Prophet, and many other things. It is the same with all other religions. Whether these prescriptions are good or bad, they are prescriptions which exact the performance of certain actions. Pseudo-Christianity alone prescribes nothing. There is nothing that a Christian is obliged to observe except fasts and prayers, which the Church itself does not recognize as obligatory. All that is necessary to the pseudo-Christian is the sacrament. But the sacrament is not fulfilled by the believer; it is administered to him by others. The pseudo-Christian is obliged to do nothing or to abstain from nothing for his own salvation, since the Church administers to him everything of which he has need. The Church baptizes him, anoints him, gives him the eucharist, confesses him, even after he has lost consciousness, administers extreme unction to him, and prays for him,—and he is saved. From the time of Constantine the Christian Church has prescribed no religious duties to its adherents. It has never required that they should abstain from anything. The Christian Church has recognized and sanctioned divorce, slavery, tribunals, all earthly powers, the death penalty, and war; it has exacted nothing except a renunciation of a purpose to do evil on the occasion of baptism, and this only in

its early days: later on, when infant baptism was introduced, even this requirement was no longer observed.

The Church confesses the doctrine of Jesus in theory, but
denies it in practice. Instead of guiding the life of the world,
the Church, through affection for the world, expounds the
metaphysical doctrine of Jesus in such a way as not to de-
rive from it any obligation as to the conduct of life, any necessity for men to live differently from the way in which
they have been living. The Church has surrendered to the
world, and simply follows in the train of its victor. The
world does as it pleases, and leaves to the Church the task
of justifying its actions with explanations as to the meaning
of life. The world organizes an existence in absolute opposition to the doctrine of Jesus, and the Church endeavors to
demonstrate that men who live contrary to the doctrine of
Jesus really live in accordance with that doctrine. The final
result is that the world lives a worse than pagan existence,
and the Church not only approves, but maintains that this
existence is in exact conformity to the doctrine of Jesus.

But a time comes when the light of the true doctrine of
Jesus shines forth from the Gospels, notwithstanding the
guilty efforts of the Church to conceal it from men's eyes,
as, for instance, in prohibiting the translation of the Bible;
there comes a time when the light reaches the people, even
through the medium of sectarians and free-thinkers, and
the falsity of the doctrine of the Church is shown so clearly
that men begin to transform the method of living that the
Church has justified.

Thus men of their own accord, and in opposition to the
sanction of the Church, have abolished slavery, abolished
the divine right of emperors and popes, and are now pro-
ceeding to abolish property and the State. And the Church
cannot forbid such action because the abolition of these in-

iquities is in conformity to the Christian doctrine, that the Church preaches after having falsified.

And in this way the conduct of human life is freed from the control of the Church, and subjected to an entirely different authority. The Church retains its dogmas, but what are its dogmas worth? A metaphysical explanation can be of use only when there is a doctrine of life which it serves to make manifest. But the Church possesses only the explanation of an organization which it once sanctioned, and which no longer exists. The Church has nothing left but temples and shrines and canonicals and vestments and words.

For eighteen centuries the Church has hidden the light of Christianity behind its forms and ceremonials, and by this same light it is put to shame. The world, with an organization sanctioned by the Church, has rejected the Church in the name of the very principles of Christianity that the Church has professed. The separation between the two is complete and cannot be concealed. Everything that truly lives in the world of Europe to-day (everything not cold and dumb in hateful isolation),—everything that is living, is detached from the Church, from all churches, and has an existence independent of the Church. Let it not be said that this is true only of the decayed civilizations of Western Europe. Russia, with its millions of civilized and uncivilized Christian rationalists, who have rejected the doctrine of the Church, proves incontestably that as regards emancipation from the yoke of the Church, she is, thanks be to God, in a worse condition of decay than the rest of Europe.

All that lives is independent of the Church. The power of the State is based upon tradition, upon science, upon popular suffrage, upon brute force, upon everything except upon the Church. Wars, the relation of State with State, are governed by principles of nationality, of the balance of power, but not by the Church. The institutions established by the State frankly ignore the Church. The idea that the Church can, in these times, serve as a basis for justice or the conservation of property, is simply absurd. Science not only does not sustain the doctrine of the Church, but is, in its development, entirely hostile to the Church. Art, formerly entirely devoted to the service of the Church, has wholly forsaken the Church. It is little to say that human life is now entirely emancipated from the Church; it has now, with regard to the Church, only contempt when the Church does not interfere with human affairs, and hatred when the Church seeks to re-assert its ancient privileges. The Church is still permitted a formal existence simply because men dread to shatter the chalice that once contained the water of life. In this way only can we account, in our age, for the existence of Catholicism, of Orthodoxy, and of the different Protestant churches.

All these churches—Catholic, Orthodox, Protestant—are like so many sentinels still keeping careful watch before the prison doors, although the prisoners have long been at liberty before their eyes, and even threaten their existence. All that actually constitutes life, that is, the activity of humanity towards progress and its own welfare, socialism, communism, the new politico-economical theories, utilitarianism, the liberty and equality of all social classes, and of men and women, all the moral principles of humanity, the sanctity of work, reason, science, art,—all these that lend an impulse to the world's progress in hostility to the Church are only fragments of the doctrine which the Church has professed, and so carefully endeavored to conceal. In these times, the life of the world is entirely independent of the doctrine of the Church. The Church is left so far behind, that men no longer hear the voices of those who preach its doctrines.

This is easily to be understood because the Church still clings to an organization of the world's life, which has been forsaken, and is rapidly falling to destruction.

Imagine a number of men rowing a boat, a pilot steering. The men rely upon the pilot, and the pilot steers well; but after a time the good pilot is replaced by another, who does not steer at all. The boat moves along rapidly and easily. At first the men do not notice the negligence of the new pilot; they are only pleased to find that the boat goes along so easily. Then they discover that the new pilot is utterly useless, and they mock at him, and drive him from his place.

The matter would not be so serious if the men, in thrusting aside the unskilful pilot, did not forget that without a pilot they are likely to take a wrong course. But so it is with our Christian society. The Church has lost its control; we move smoothly onward, and we are a long way from our point of departure. Science, that especial pride of this nineteenth century, is sometimes alarmed; but that is because of the absence of a pilot. We are moving onward, but to what goal? We organize our life without in the least knowing why, or to what end. But we can no longer be contented to live without knowing why, any more than we can navigate a boat without knowing the course that we are following.

If men could do nothing of themselves, if they were not responsible for their condition, they might very reasonably reply to the question, "Why are you in this situation?"— "We do not know; but here we are, and submit." But men are the builders of their own destiny, and more especially of the destiny of their children; and so when we ask, "Why do you bring together millions of troops, and why do you make soldiers of yourselves, and mangle and murder one another? Why have you expended, and why do you still expend, an enormous sum of human energy in the construction of useless and unhealthful cities? Why do you organize ridiculous tribunals, and send people whom you consider as criminals from France to Cayenne, from Russia to Siberia, from England to Australia, when you know the hopeless folly of it? Why do you abandon agriculture, which you love, for work in factories and mills, which you despise? Why do you bring up your children in a way that will force them to lead an existence which you find worthless? Why do you do this?" To all these questions men feel obliged to make some reply.

If this existence were an agreeable one, and men took pleasure in it, even then men would try to explain why they continued to live under such conditions. But all these things are terribly difficult; they are endured with murmuring and painful struggles, and men cannot refrain from reflecting upon the motive which impels them to such a course. They must cease to maintain the accepted organization of existence, or they must explain why they give it their support. And so men never have allowed this question to pass unanswered. We find in all ages some attempt at a response. The Jew lived as he lived, that is, made war, put criminals to death, built the Temple, organized his entire existence in one way and not another, because, as he was convinced, he thereby followed the laws which God himself had promulgated. We may say the same of the Hindu, the Chinaman, the Roman, and the Mohammedan. A similar response was given by the Christian a century ago, and is given by the great mass of Christians now.

A century ago, and among the ignorant now, the nominal Christian makes this reply: "Compulsory military service, wars, tribunals, and the death penalty, all exist in obedience to the law of God transmitted to us by the Church. This is a fallen world. All the evil that exists, exists by God's will, as a punishment for the sins of men. For this reason we can do nothing to palliate evil. We can only save our own souls by faith, by the sacraments, by prayers, and by submission to the will of God as transmitted by the Church. The Church teaches us that all Christians should unhesitatingly obey their rulers, who are the Lord's anointed, and obey also persons placed in authority by rulers; that they ought to defend their property and that of others by force, wage war, inflict the death penalty, and in all things submit to the authorities, who command by the will of God."

Whatever we may think of the reasonableness of these explanations, they once sufficed for a believing Christian, as similar explanations satisfied a Jew or a Mohammedan, and men were not obliged to renounce all reason for living according to a law which they recognized as divine. But in this time only the most ignorant people have faith in any such explanations, and the number of these diminishes every day and every hour. It is impossible to check this tendency. Men irresistibly follow those who lead the way, and sooner or later must pass over the same ground as the advance guard. The advance guard is now in a critical position; those who compose it organize life to suit themselves, prepare the same conditions for those who are to follow, and absolutely have not the slightest idea of why they do so. No civilized man in the vanguard of progress is able to give any reply now to the direct questions, "Why do you lead the life that you do lead? Why do you establish the conditions that you do establish?" I have propounded these questions to hundreds of people, and never have got from them a direct reply. Instead of a direct reply to the direct question, I have received in return a response to a question that I had not asked.

When we ask a Catholic, or Protestant, or Orthodox believer why he leads an existence contrary to the doctrine of Jesus, instead of making a direct response he begins to speak of the melancholy state of scepticism characteristic of this generation, of evil-minded persons who spread doubt broadcast among the masses, of the importance of the future of the existing Church. But he will not tell you why he does not act in conformity to the commands of the religion that he professes. Instead of speaking of his own condition, he will talk to you about the condition of humanity in general, and of that of the Church, as if his own life were not of the slightest significance, and his sole preoccupations were the salvation of humanity, and of what he calls the Church.

A philosopher of whatever school he may be, whether an idealist or a spiritualist, a pessimist or a positivist, if we ask of him why he lives as he lives, that is to say, in disaccord with his philosophical doctrine, will begin at once to talk about the progress of humanity and about the historical law of this progress which he has discovered, and in virtue of which humanity gravitates toward righteousness. But he never will make any direct reply to the question why he himself, on his own account, does not live in harmony with what he recognizes as the dictates of reason. It would seem as if the philosopher were as preoccupied as the believer, not with his personal life, but with observing the effect of general laws upon the development of humanity.

The "average" man (that is, one of the immense majority of civilized people who are half sceptics and half believers, and who all, without exception, deplore existence, condemn its organization, and predict universal destruction),—the average man, when we ask him why he continues to lead a life that he condemns, without making any effort towards its amelioration, makes no direct reply, but begins at once to talk about things in general, about justice, about the State, about commerce, about civilization. If he be a member of the police or a prosecuting attorney, he asks, "And what would become of the State, if I, to ameliorate my existence, were to cease to serve it?" "What would become of commerce?" is his demand if he be a merchant; "What of civilization, if I cease to work for it, and seek only to better my own condition?" will be the objection of another. His response always will be in this form, as if the duty of his life were not to seek the good conformable to his nature, but to serve the State, or commerce, or civilization.

The average man replies in just the same manner as does the believer or the philosopher. Instead of making the question a personal one, he glides at once to generalities. This subterfuge is employed simply because the believer and the philosopher, and the average man have no positive doctrine concerning existence, and cannot, therefore, reply to the personal question, "What of your own life?" They are disgusted and humiliated at not possessing the slightest trace of a doctrine with regard to life, for no one can live in peace without some understanding of what life really means. But nowadays only Christians cling to a fantastic and worn-out creed as an explanation of why life is as it is, and is not otherwise. Only Christians give the name of religion to a system which is not of the least use to any one. Only among Christians is life separated from any or all doctrine, and left without any definition whatever. Moreover, science, like tradition, has formulated from the fortuitous and abnormal condition of humanity a general law. Learned men, such as Tiele and Spencer, treat religion as a serious matter, understanding by religion the metaphysical doctrine of the universal principle, without suspecting that they have lost sight of religion as a whole by confining their attention entirely to one of its phases.

From all this we get very extraordinary results. We see learned and intelligent men artlessly believing that they are emancipated from all religion simply because they reject the metaphysical explanation of the universal principle which satisfied a former generation. It does not occur to them that men cannot live without some theory of existence; that every human being lives according to some principle, and that this principle by which he governs his life is his religion. The people of whom we have been speaking are persuaded that they have reasonable convictions, but that they have no religion. Nevertheless, however serious their asseverations, they have a religion from the moment that they undertake to govern their actions by reason, for a reasonable act is determined by some sort of faith. Now their faith is in what they are told to do. The faith of those who deny religion is in a religion of obedience to the will of the ruling majority; in a word, submission to established authority.

We may live a purely animal life according to the doctrine of the world, without recognizing any controlling motive more binding than the rules of established authority. But he who lives this way cannot affirm that he lives a reasonable life. Before affirming that we live a reasonable life, we must determine what is the doctrine of the life which we regard as reasonable. Alas! wretched men that we are, we possess not the semblance of any such doctrine, and more than that, we have lost all perception of the necessity for a reasonable doctrine of life.

Ask the believers or sceptics of this age, what doctrine of life they follow. They will be obliged to confess that they follow but one doctrine, the doctrine based upon laws formulated by the judiciary or by legislative assemblies, and enforced by the police—the favorite doctrine of most Europeans. They know that this doctrine does not come from on high, or from prophets, or from sages; they are continually finding fault with the laws drawn up by the judiciary or formulated by legislative assemblies, but nevertheless they submit to the police charged with their enforcement. They submit without murmuring to the most terrible exactions. The clerks employed by the judiciary or the legislative assemblies decree by statute that every young man must be ready to take up arms, to kill others, and to die himself, and that all parents who have adult sons must favor obedience to this law which was drawn up yesterday by a mercenary official, and may be revoked to-morrow.

We have lost sight of the idea that a law may be in itself reasonable, and binding upon every one in spirit as well as in letter. The Hebrews possessed a law which regulated life, not by forced obedience to its requirements, but by appealing to the conscience of each individual; and the existence of this law is considered as an exceptional attribute of the Hebrew people. That the Hebrews should have been willing to obey only what they recognized by spiritual perception as the incontestable truth direct from God is considered a remarkable national trait. But it appears that the natural and normal state of civilized men is to obey what to their own knowledge is decreed by despicable officials and enforced by the co-operation of armed police.

The distinctive trait of civilized man is to obey what the majority of men regard as iniquitous, contrary to conscience. I seek in vain in civilized society as it exists to-day for any clearly formulated moral bases of life. There are none. No perception of their necessity exists. On the contrary, we find the extraordinary conviction that they are superfluous; that religion is nothing more than a few words about God and a future life, and a few ceremonies very useful for the salvation of the soul according to some, and good for nothing according to others; but that life happens of itself and has no need of any fundamental rule, and that we have only to do what we are told to do.

The two substantial sources of faith, the doctrine that governs life, and the explanation of the meaning of life, are regarded as of very unequal value. The first is considered as of very little importance, and as having no relation to faith whatever; the second, as the explanation of a bygone state of existence, or as made up of speculations concerning the historical development of life, is considered as of great significance. As to all that constitutes the life of man expressed in action, the members of our modern society depend willingly for guidance upon people who, like themselves, know not why they direct their fellows to live in one way and not in another. This disposition holds good whether the question at issue is to decide whether to kill or not to kill, to judge or not to judge, to bring up children in this way or in that. And men look upon an existence like this as reasonable, and have no feeling of shame!

The explanations of the Church which pass for faith, and the true faith of our generation, which is in obedience to social laws and the laws of the State, have reached a stage of sharp antagonism. The majority of civilized people have nothing to regulate life but faith in the police. This condition would be unbearable if it were universal. Fortunately there is a remnant, made up of the noblest minds of the age, who are not contented with this religion, but have an entirely different faith with regard to what the life of man ought to be. These men are looked upon as the most malevolent, the most dangerous, and generally as the most unbelieving of all human beings, and yet they are the only men of our time believing in the Gospel doctrine, if not as a whole, at least in part. These people, as a general thing, know little of the doctrine of Jesus; they do not understand it, and, like their adversaries, they refuse to accept the leading principle of the religion of Jesus, which is to resist not evil; often they have nothing but a hatred for the name of Jesus; but their whole faith with regard to what life ought to be is unconsciously based upon the humane and eternal truths comprised in the Christian doctrine. This remnant, in spite of calumny and persecution, are the only ones who do not tamely submit to the orders of the first comer. Consequently they are the only ones in these days who live a reasonable and not an animal life, the only ones who have faith.

The connecting link between the world and the Church, although carefully cherished by the Church, becomes more and more attenuated. To-day it is little more than a hindrance. The union between the Church and the world has no longer any justification. The mysterious process of maturation is going on before our eyes. The connecting bond will soon be severed, and the vital social organism will begin to exercise its functions as a wholly independent existence. The doctrine of the Church, with its dogmas, its councils, and its hierarchy, is manifestly united to the doctrine of Jesus. The connecting link is as perceptible as the cord which binds the newly-born child to its mother; but as the umbilical cord and the placenta become after parturition useless pieces of flesh, which are carefully buried out of regard for what they once nourished, so the Church has become a useless organism, to be preserved, if at all, in some museum of curiosities out of regard for what it has once been. As soon as respiration and circulation are established, the former source of nutrition becomes a hindrance to life. Vain and foolish would it be to attempt to retain the bond, and to force the child that has come into the light of day to receive its nourishment by a pre-natal process. But the deliverance of the child from the maternal tie does not ensure life. The life of the newly born depends upon another bond of union which is established between it and its mother that its nourishment may be maintained.

And so it must be with our Christian world of to-day. The doctrine of Jesus has brought the world into the light. The Church, one of the organs of the doctrine of Jesus, has fulfilled its mission and is now useless. The world cannot be bound to the Church; but the deliverance of the world from the Church will not ensure life. Life will begin when the world perceives its own weakness and the necessity for a different source of strength. The Christian world feels this necessity: it proclaims its helplessness, it feels the impossibility of depending upon its former means of nourishment, the inadequacy of any other form of nourishment except that of the doctrine by which it was brought forth. This modern European world of ours, apparently so sure of itself, so bold, so decided, and within so preyed upon by terror and despair, is exactly in the situation of a newly born animal: it writhes, it cries aloud, it is perplexed, it knows not what to do; it feels that its former source of nourishment is withdrawn, but it knows not where to seek for another. A newly born lamb shakes its head, opens its eyes and looks about, and leaps, and bounds, and would make us think by its apparently intelligent movements that it already has mastered the secret of living; but of this the poor little creature knows nothing. The impetuosity and energy it displays were drawn from its mother through a medium of transmission that has just been broken, nevermore to be renewed. The situation of the new comer is one of delight, and at the same time is full of peril. It is animated by youth and strength, but it is lost if it cannot avail itself of the nourishment only to be had from its mother.

And so it is with our European world. What complex activities, what energy, what intelligence, does it apparently possess! It would seem as if all its deeds were governed by reason. With what enthusiasm, what vigor, what youthfulness do the denizens of this modern world manifest their abounding vitality! The arts and sciences, the various industries, political and administrative details, all are full of life. But this life is due to inspiration received through the connecting link that binds it to its source. The Church, by transmitting the truth of the doctrine of Jesus, has communicated life to the world. Upon this nourishment the world has grown and developed. But the Church has had its day and is now superfluous.

The world is possessed of a living organism; the means by which it formerly received its nourishment has withered away, and it has not yet found another; and it seeks everywhere, everywhere but at the true source of life. It still possesses the animation derived from nourishment already received, and it does not yet understand that its future nourishment is only to be had from one source, and by its own efforts. The world must now understand that the period of gestation is ended, and that a new process of conscious nutrition must henceforth maintain its life. The truth of the doctrine of Jesus, once unconsciously absorbed by humanity through the organism of the Church, must now be consciously recognized; for in the truth of this doctrine humanity has always obtained its vital force. Men must lift up the torch of truth, which has so long remained concealed, and carry it before them, guiding their actions by its light.

The doctrine of Jesus, as a religion that governs the actions of men and explains to them the meaning of life, is now before the world just as it was eighteen hundred years ago. Formerly the world had the explanations of the Church which, in concealing the doctrine, seemed in itself to offer a satisfactory interpretation of life; but now the time is come when the Church has lost its usefulness, and the world, having no other means for sustaining its true existence, can only feel its helplessness and go for aid directly to the doctrine of Jesus.

Now, Jesus first taught men to believe in the light, and that the light is within themselves. Jesus taught men to lift on high the light of reason. He taught them to live, guiding their actions by this light, and to do nothing contrary to reason. It is unreasonable, it is foolish, to go out to kill Turks or Germans; it is unreasonable to make use of the labor of others that you and yours may be clothed in the height of fashion and maintain that mortal source of ennui, a salon; it is unreasonable to take people already corrupted by idleness and depravity and shut them up within prison walls, and thereby devote them to an existence of absolute idleness and depravation; it is unreasonable to live in the pestilential air of cities when a purer atmosphere is within your reach; it is unreasonable to base the education of your children on the grammatical laws of dead languages;—all this is unreasonable, and yet it is to-day the life of the European world, which lives a life of no meaning; which acts, but acts without a purpose, having no confidence in reason, and existing in opposition to its decrees.

The doctrine of Jesus is the light. The light shines forth, and the darkness cannot conceal it. Men cannot deny it, men cannot refuse to accept its guidance. They must depend on the doctrine of Jesus, which penetrates among all the errors with which the life of men is surrounded. Like the insensible ether filling universal space, enveloping all created things, so the doctrine of Jesus is inevitable for every man in whatever situation he may be found. Men cannot refuse to recognize the doctrine of Jesus; they may deny the metaphysical explanation of life which it gives (we may deny everything), but the doctrine of Jesus alone offers rules for the conduct of life without which humanity has never lived, and never will be able to live; without which no human being has lived or can live, if he would live as man should live,—a reasonable life. The power of the doctrine of Jesus is not in its explanation of the meaning of life, but in the rules that it gives for the conduct of life.

The metaphysical doctrine of Jesus is not new; it is that eternal doctrine of humanity inscribed in all the hearts of men, and preached by all the prophets of all the ages. The power of the doctrine of Jesus is in the application of this metaphysical doctrine to life.

The metaphysical basis of the ancient doctrine of the Hebrews, which enjoined love to God and men, is identical with the metaphysical basis of the doctrine of Jesus. But the application of this doctrine to life, as expounded by Moses, was very different from the teachings of Jesus. The Hebrews, in applying the Mosaic law to life, were obliged to fulfil six hundred and thirteen commandments, many of which were absurd and cruel, and yet all were based upon the authority of the Scriptures. The doctrine of life, as given by Jesus upon the same metaphysical basis, is expressed in five reasonable and beneficent commandments, having an obvious and justifiable meaning, and embracing within their restrictions the whole of human life. A Jew, a disciple of Confucius, a Buddhist, or a Mohammedan, who sincerely doubts the truth of his own religion, cannot refuse to accept the doctrine of Jesus; much less, then, can this doctrine be rejected by the Christian world of to-day, which is now living without any moral law. The doctrine of Jesus cannot interfere in any way with the manner in which men of to-day regard the world; it is, to begin with, in harmony with their metaphysics, but it gives them what they have not now, what is indispensable to their existence, and what they all seek,—it offers them a way of life; not an unknown way, but a way already explored and familiar to all.

Let us suppose that you are a sincere Christian, it matters not of what confession. You believe in the creation of the world, in the Trinity, in the fall and redemption of man, in the sacraments, in prayer, in the Church. The doctrine of Jesus is not opposed to your dogmatic belief, and is absolutely in harmony with your theory of the origin of the universe; and it offers you something that you do not possess. While you retain your present religion you feel that your own life and the life of the world is full of evil that you know not how to remedy. The doctrine of Jesus (which should be binding upon you since it is the doctrine of your own God) offers you simple and practical rules which will surely deliver you, you and your fellows, from the evils with which you are tormented.

Believe, if you will, in paradise, in hell, in the pope, in the Church, in the sacraments, in the redemption; pray according to the dictates of your faith, attend upon your devotions, sing your hymns,—but all this will not prevent you from practising the five commandments given by Jesus for your welfare: Be not angry ; Do not commit adultery; Take no oaths; Resist not evil; Do not make war. It may happen that you will break one of these rules; you will perhaps yield to temptation, and violate one of them, just as you violate the rules of your present religion, or the articles of the civil code, or the laws of custom. In the same way you may, perhaps, in moments of temptation, fail of observing all the commandments of Jesus. But, in that case, do not calmly sit down as you do now, and so organize your existence as to render it a task of extreme difficulty not to be angry, not to commit adultery, not to take oaths, not to resist evil, not to make war; organize rather an existence which shall render the doing of all these things as difficult as the non-performance of them is now laborious. You cannot refuse to recognize the validity of these rules, for they are the commandments of the God whom you pretend to worship.

Let us suppose that you are an unbeliever, a philosopher, it matters not of what special school. You affirm that the progress of the world is in accordance with a law that you have discovered. The doctrine of Jesus does not oppose

your views; it is in harmony with the law that you have discovered. But, aside from this law, in pursuance of which the
world will in the course of a thousand years reach a state of
felicity, there is still your own personal life to be considered.
This life you can use by living in conformity to reason, or
you can waste it by living in opposition to reason, and you
have now for its guidance no rule whatever, except the decrees drawn up by men whom you do not esteem, and enforced by the police. The doctrine of Jesus offers you rules
which are assuredly in accord with your law of "altruism,"
which is nothing but a feeble paraphrase of this same doctrine of Jesus.

Let us suppose that you are an average man, half sceptic,
half believer, one who has no time to analyze the meaning
of human life, and one therefore who has no determinate
theory of existence. You live as lives the rest of the world
about you. The doctrine of Jesus is not at all contrary to
your condition. You are incapable of reason, of verifying the
truths of the doctrines that are taught you; it is easier for
you to do as others do. But however modest may be your
estimate of your powers of reason, you know that you have
within you a judge that sometimes approves your acts and
sometimes condemns them. However modest your social
position, there are occasions when you are bound to reflect
and ask yourself, "Shall I follow the example of the rest of
the world, or shall I act in accordance with my own judgment?" It is precisely on these occasions when you are
called upon to solve some problem with regard to the conduct of life, that the commandments of Jesus appeal to you
in all their efficiency. The commandments of Jesus will
surely respond to your inquiry, because they apply to your
whole existence. The response will be in accord with your
reason and your conscience. If you are nearer to faith than
to unbelief, you will, in following these commandments,

act in harmony with the will of God. If you are nearer to scepticism than to belief, you will, in following the doctrine of Jesus, govern your actions by the laws of reason, for the commandments of Jesus make manifest their own meaning, and their own justification.

"Now is the judgment of this world: now shall the prince of this world be cast out." (John xii. 31.)

"These things have I spoken unto you, that in me ye may have peace. In the world ye have tribulation: but be of good cheer; I have overcome the world." (John xvi. 33.)

The world, that is, the evil in the world, is overcome. If evil still exists in the world, it exists only through the influence of inertia; it no longer contains the principle of vitality. For those who have faith in the commandments of Jesus, it does not exist at all. It is vanquished by an awakened conscience, by the elevation of the son of man. A train that has been put in motion continues to move in the direction in which it was started; but the time comes when the intelligent effort of a controlling hand is made manifest, and the movement is reversed.

"Ye are of God, and have overcome them because greater is he that is within you than he that is in the world." (1 John v. 4.)

The faith that triumphs over the doctrines of the world is faith in the doctrine of Jesus.

VII

I BELIEVE in the doctrine of Jesus, and this is my religion:—

I believe that nothing but the fulfilment of the doctrine of Jesus can give true happiness to men. I believe that the fulfilment of this doctrine is possible, easy, and pleasant. I believe that although none other follows this doctrine, and I alone am left to practise it, I cannot refuse to obey it, if I would save my life from the certainty of eternal loss; just as a man in a burning house if he find a door of safety, must go out, so I must avail myself of the way to salvation. I believe that my life according to the doctrine of the world has been a torment, and that a life according to the doctrine of Jesus can alone give me in this world the happiness for which I was destined by the Father of Life. I believe that this doctrine is essential to the welfare of humanity, will save me from the certainty of eternal loss, and will give me in this world the greatest possible sum of happiness. Believing thus, I am obliged to practise its commandments.

"The law was given by Moses; grace and truth came by Jesus Christ." (John i. 17.)

The doctrine of Jesus is a doctrine of grace and truth. Once I knew not grace and knew not truth. Mistaking evil for good, I fell into evil, and I doubted the righteousness of my tendency toward good. I understand and believe now that the good toward which I was attracted is the will of the Father, the essence of life.

Jesus has told us to live in pursuit of the good, and to be-

ware of snares and temptations (σκάνδαλον) which, by en-
ticing us with the semblance of good, draw us away from
true goodness, and lead us into evil. He has taught us that
our welfare is to be sought in fellowship with all men; that
evil is a violation of fellowship with the son of man, and
that we must not deprive ourselves of the welfare to be had
by obedience to his doctrine.

Jesus has demonstrated that fellowship with the son of
man, the love of men for one another, is not merely an ideal
after which men are to strive; he has shown us that this love
and this fellowship are natural attributes of men in their
normal condition, the condition into which children are
born, the condition in which all men would live if they were
not drawn aside by error, illusions, and temptations.

In his commandments, Jesus has enumerated clearly and
unmistakably the temptations that interfere with this natural condition of love and fellowship and render it a prey to
evil. The commandments of Jesus offer the remedies by
which I must save myself from the temptations that have
deprived me of happiness; and so I am forced to believe
that these commandments are true. Happiness was within
my grasp and I destroyed it. In his commandments Jesus
has shown me the temptations that lead to the destruction
of happiness. I can no longer work for the destruction of my
happiness, and in this determination, and in this alone, is
the substance of my religion.

Jesus has shown me that the first temptation destructive
of happiness is enmity toward men, anger against them. I
cannot refuse to believe this, and so I cannot willingly remain at enmity with others. I cannot, as I could once, foster
anger, be proud of it, fan it into flame, justify it, regarding
myself as an intelligent and superior man and others as
useless and foolish people. Now, when I give up to anger, I

can only realize that I alone am guilty, and seek to make peace with those who have aught against me.

But this is not all. While I now see that anger is an abnormal, pernicious, and morbid state, I also perceive the temptation that led me into it. The temptation was in separating myself from my fellows, recognizing only a few of them as my equals, and regarding all the others as persons of no account *(rekim)* or as uncultivated animals *(fools)*. I see now that this wilful separation from other men, this judgment of *raca* or *fool* passed upon others, was the principal source of my disagreements. In looking over my past life I saw that I had rarely permitted my anger to rise against those whom I considered as my equals, whom I seldom abused. But the least disagreeable action on the part of one whom I considered an inferior inflamed my anger and led me to abusive words or actions, and the more superior I felt myself to be, the less careful I was of my temper; sometimes the mere supposition that a man was of a lower social position than myself was enough to provoke me to an outrageous manner.

I understand now that he alone is above others who is humble with others and makes himself the servant of all. I understand now why those that are great in the sight of men are an abomination to God, who has declared woe upon the rich and mighty and invoked blessedness upon the poor and humble. Now I understand this truth, I have faith in it, and this faith has transformed my perception of what is right and important, and what is wrong and despicable. Everything that once seemed to me right and important, such as honors, glory, civilization, wealth, the complications and refinements of existence, luxury, rich food, fine clothing, etiquette, have become for me wrong and despicable. Everything that formerly seemed to me wrong and despicable, such as rusticity, obscurity, poverty, austerity, simplicity of surroundings, of food, of clothing, of manners, all have now become right and important to me. And so although I may at times give myself up to anger and abuse another, I cannot deliberately yield to wrath and so deprive myself of the true source of happiness,—fellowship and love; for it is possible that a man should lay a snare for his own feet and so be lost. Now, I can no longer give my support to anything that lifts me above or separates me from others. I cannot, as I once did, recognize in myself or others titles or ranks or qualities aside from the title and quality of manhood. I can no longer seek for fame and glory; I can no longer cultivate a system of instruction which separates me from men. I cannot in my surroundings, my food, my clothing, my manners, strive for what not only separates me from others but renders me a reproach to the majority of mankind.

Jesus showed me another temptation destructive of happiness, that is, debauchery, the desire to possess another woman than her to whom I am united. I can no longer, as I did once, consider my sensuality as a sublime trait of human nature. I can no longer justify it by my love for the beautiful, or my amorousness, or the faults of my companion. At the first inclination toward debauchery I cannot fail to recognize that I am in a morbid and abnormal state, and to seek to rid myself of the besetting sin.

Knowing that debauchery is an evil, I also know its cause, and can thus evade it. I know now that the principal cause of this temptation is not the necessity for the sexual relation, but the abandonment of wives by their husbands, and of husbands by their wives. I know now that a man who forsakes a woman, or a woman who forsakes a man, when the two have once been united, is guilty of the divorce which Jesus forbade, because men and women aban-

doned by their first companions are the original cause of all
the debauchery in the world.

In seeking to discover the influences that led to debauchery, I found one to be a barbarous physical and intellectual
education that developed the erotic passion which the
world endeavors to justify by the most subtile arguments.
But the principal influence I found to be the abandonment
of the woman to whom I had first been united, and the situation of the abandoned women around me. The principal
source of temptation was not in carnal desires, but in the
fact that those desires were not satisfied in the men and
women by whom I was surrounded. I now understand the
words of Jesus when he says:—

*"He which made them from the beginning, made them male
and female. . . . So that they are no more twain, but one flesh.
What, therefore, God hath joined together, let not man put asun-
der."* (Matt. xix. 4–6.)

I understand now that monogamy is the natural law of
humanity, which cannot with impunity be violated. I now
understand perfectly the words declaring that the man or
woman who separates from a companion to seek another,
forces the forsaken one to resort to debauchery, and thus introduces into the world an evil that returns upon those who
cause it.

This I believe; and the faith I now have has transformed
my opinions with regard to the right and important, and
the wrong and despicable, things of life. What once seemed
to me the most delightful existence in the world, an existence made up of dainty, aesthetic pleasures and passions,
is now revolting to me. And a life of simplicity and indi-
gence, which moderates the sexual desires, now seems to
me good. The human institution of marriage, which gives a
nominal sanction to the union of man and woman, I regard
as of less grave importance than that the union, when ac-

complished, should be regarded as the will of God, and never be broken.

Now, when in moments of weakness I yield to the promptings of desire, I know the snare that would deliver me into evil, and so I cannot deliberately plan my method of existence as formerly I was accustomed to do. I no longer habitually cherish physical sloth and luxury, which excite to excessive sensuality. I can no longer pursue amusements which are oil to the fire of amorous sensuality,—the reading of romances and the most of poetry, listening to music, attendance at theatres and balls,—amusements that once seemed to me elevated and refining, but which I now see to be injurious. I can no longer abandon the woman with whom I have been united, for I know that by forsaking her, I set a snare for myself, for her, and for others. I can no longer encourage the gross and idle existence of others. I can no longer encourage or take part in licentious pastimes, romantic literature, plays, operas, balls, which are so many snares for myself and for others. I cannot favor the celibacy of persons fitted for the marriage relation. I cannot encourage the separation of wives from their husbands. I cannot make any distinction between unions that are called by the name of marriage, and those that are denied this name. I am obliged to consider as sacred and absolute the sole and unique union by which man is once for all indissolubly bound to the first woman with whom he has been united.

Jesus has shown me that the third temptation destructive to true happiness is the oath. I am obliged to believe his words; consequently, I cannot, as I once did, bind myself by oath to serve any one for any purpose, and I can no longer, as I did formerly, justify myself for having taken an oath because "it would harm no one," because everybody did the same, because it is necessary for the State, because the consequences might be bad for me or for some one else if I refuse to submit to this exaction. I know now that it is an evil for myself and for others, and I cannot conform to it.

Nor is this all. I now know the snare that led me into evil, and I can no longer act as an accomplice. I know that the snare is in the use of God's name to sanction an imposture, and that the imposture consists in promising in advance to obey the commands of one man, or of many men, while I ought to obey the commands of God alone. I know now that evils the most terrible of all in their result—war, imprisonments, capital punishment—exist only because of the oath, in virtue of which men make themselves instruments of evil, and believe that they free themselves from all responsibility. As I think now of the many evils that have impelled me to hostility and hatred, I see that they all originated with the oath, the engagement to submit to the will of others. I understand now the meaning of the words:—

"But let your speech be, Yea, yea; nay, nay; and whatsoever is more than these is of evil." (Matt. v. 37.)

Understanding this, I am convinced that the oath is destructive of my true welfare and of that of others, and this belief changes my estimate of right and wrong, of the important and despicable. What once seemed to me right and important,—the promise of fidelity to the government supported by the oath, the exacting of oaths from others, and all acts contrary to conscience, done because of the oath, now seem to me wrong and despicable. Therefore I can no longer evade the commandment of Jesus forbidding the oath, I can no longer bind myself by oath to any one, I cannot exact an oath from another, I cannot encourage men to take an oath, or to cause others to take an oath; nor can I regard the oath as necessary, important, or even inoffensive.

Jesus has shown me that the fourth temptation destructive to my happiness is the resort to violence for the resistance of evil. I am obliged to believe that this is an evil for myself and for others; consequently, I cannot, as I did once, deliberately resort to violence, and seek to justify my action with the pretext that it is indispensable for the defence of my person and property, or of the persons and property of others. I can no longer yield to the first impulse to resort to violence; I am obliged to renounce it, and to abstain from it altogether.

But this is not all. I understand now the snare that caused me to fall into this evil. I know now that the snare consisted in the erroneous belief that my life could be made secure by violence, by the defence of my person and property against the encroachments of others. I know now that a great portion of the evils that afflict mankind are due to this,—that men, instead of giving their work for others, deprive themselves completely of the privilege of work, and forcibly appropriate the labor of their fellows. Every one regards a resort to violence as the best possible security for life and for property, and I now see that a great portion of the evil that I did myself, and saw others do, resulted from this practice. I understood now the meaning of the words:—

"Not to be ministered unto, but to minister." "The laborer is worthy of his food."

I believe now that my true welfare, and that of others, is possible only when I labor not for myself, but for another, and that I must not refuse to labor for another, but to give with joy that of which he has need. This faith has changed my estimate of what is right and important, and wrong and despicable. What once seemed to me right and important— riches, proprietary rights, the point of honor, the maintenance of personal dignity and personal privileges—have now become to me wrong and despicable. Labor for others, poverty, humility, the renunciation of property and of personal privileges, have become in my eyes right and important.

When, now, in a moment of forgetfulness, I yield to the impulse to resort to violence, for the defence of my person or property, or of the persons or property of others, I can no longer deliberately make use of this snare for my own destruction and the destruction of others. I can no longer acquire property. I can no longer resort to force in any form for my own defence or the defence of another. I can no longer co-operate with any power whose object is the defence of men and their property by violence. I can no longer act in a judicial capacity, or clothe myself with any authority, or take part in the exercise of any jurisdiction whatever. I can no longer encourage others in the support of tribunals, or in the exercise of authoritative administration.

Jesus has shown me that the fifth temptation that deprives me of well-being, is the distinction that we make between compatriots and foreigners. I must believe this; consequently, if, in a moment of forgetfulness, I have a feeling of hostility toward a man of another nationality, I am obliged, in moments of reflection, to regard this feeling as wrong. I can no longer, as I did formerly, justify my hostility by the superiority of my own people over others, or by the ignorance, the cruelty, or the barbarism of another race. I can no longer refrain from striving to be even more friendly with a foreigner than with one of my own countrymen.

I know now that the distinction I once made between my own people and those of other countries is destructive of my welfare; but, more than this, I now know the snare that led me into this evil, and I can no longer, as I did once, walk deliberately and calmly into this snare. I know now that this snare consists in the erroneous belief that my welfare is dependent only upon the welfare of my countrymen, and not upon the welfare of all mankind. I know now that my fellowship with others cannot be shut off by a frontier, or by a government decree which decides that I belong to some particular political organization. I know now that all men are everywhere brothers and equals. When I think now of all the evil that I have done, that I have endured, and that I have seen about me, arising from national enmities, I see clearly that it is all due to that gross imposture called patriotism,—love for one's native land. When I think now of my education, I see how these hateful feelings were grafted into my mind. I understand now the meaning of the words:—

"Love your enemies, and pray for them that persecute you; that ye may be sons of your Father that is in heaven: for he maketh his sun to rise on the evil and the good, and sendeth rain on the just and the unjust."

I understand now that true welfare is possible for me only on condition that I recognize my fellowship with the whole world. I believe this, and the belief has changed my estimate of what is right and wrong, important and despicable. What once seemed to me right and important—love of country, love for those of my own race, for the organization called the State, services rendered at the expense of the welfare of other men, military exploits—now seem to me detestable and pitiable. What once seemed to me shameful and wrong—renunciation of nationality, and the cultivation of cosmopolitanism—now seem to me right and important. When, now, in a moment of forgetfulness, I sustain a Russian in preference to a foreigner, and desire the success of Russia or of the Russian people, I can no longer in lucid moments allow myself to be controlled by illusions so destructive to my welfare and the welfare of others. I can no longer recognize states or peoples; I can no longer take part in any difference between peoples or states, or any discussion between them either oral or written, much less in any service in behalf of any particular state. I can no longer co-operate with measures maintained by divisions between states,— the collection of custom duties, taxes, the manufacture of arms and projectiles, or any act favoring armaments, military service, and, for a stronger reason, wars,—neither can I encourage others to take any part in them.

I understand in what my true welfare consists, I have faith in that, and consequently I cannot do what would inevitably be destructive of that welfare. I not only have faith that I ought to live thus, but I have faith that if I live thus, and only thus, my life will attain its only possible meaning, and be reasonable, pleasant, and indestructible by death. I believe that my reasonable life, the light I bear with me, was given to me only that it might shine before men, not in words only, but in good deeds, that men may thereby glorify the Father. I believe that my life and my consciousness of truth is the talent confided to me for a good purpose, and that this talent fulfils its mission only when it is of use to others. I believe that I am a Ninevite with regard to other Jonahs from whom I have learned and shall learn of the truth; but that I am a Jonah in regard to other Ninevites to whom I am bound to transmit the truth. I believe that the only meaning of my life is to be attained by living in accordance with the light that is within me, and that I must allow this light to shine forth to be seen of all men. This faith gives me renewed strength to fulfil the doctrine of Jesus, and to overcome the obstacles which still arise in my pathway. All that once caused me to doubt the possibility of practising the doctrine of Jesus, everything that once turned me aside, the possibility of privations, and of suffering, and death, inflicted by those who know not the doctrine of Jesus, now confirm its truth and draw me into its service. Jesus said, *"When you have lifted up the son of man, then shall you know that I am he,"*—then shall you be drawn into my service,— and I feel that I am irresistibly drawn to him by the influence of his doctrine. *"The truth,"* he says again, *"The truth shall make you free,"* and I know that I am in perfect liberty.

I once thought that if a foreign invasion occurred, or even if evil-minded persons attacked me, and I did not defend myself, I should be robbed and beaten and tortured and killed with those whom I felt bound to protect, and this possibility troubled me. But this that once troubled me now seems desirable and in conformity with the truth. I know now that the foreign enemy and the malefactors or brigands are all men like myself; that, like myself, they love good and hate evil; that they live as I live, on the borders of death; and that, with me, they seek for salvation, and will find it in the doctrine of Jesus. The evil that they do to me will be evil to them, and so can be nothing but good for me. But if truth is unknown to them, and they do evil thinking that they do good, I, who know the truth, am bound to reveal it to them, and this I can do only by refusing to participate in evil, and thereby confessing the truth by my example.

"But hither come the enemy,—Germans, Turks, savages; if you do not make war on them, they will exterminate you!" They will do nothing of the sort. If there were a society of Christian men that did evil to none and gave of their labor for the good of others, such a society would have no enemies to kill or to torture them. The foreigners would take only what the members of this society voluntarily gave, making no distinction between Russians, or Turks, or Germans. But when Christians live in the midst of a non-Christian society which defends itself by force of arm, and calls upon the Christians to join in waging war, then the Christians have an opportunity for revealing the truth to them who know it not. A Christian knowing the truth bears witness of the truth before others, and this testimony can be made manifest only by example. He must renounce war and do good to all men, whether they are foreigners or compatriots.

"But there are wicked men among compatriots; they will attack a Christian, and if the latter do not defend himself, will pillage and massacre him and his family." No; they will not do so. If all the members of this family are Christians, and consequently hold their lives only for the service of others, no man will be found insane enough to deprive such people of the necessaries of life or to kill them. The famous Maclay lived among the most bloodthirsty of savages; they did not kill him, they reverenced him and followed his teachings, simply because he did not fear them, exacted nothing from them, and treated them always with kindness.

"But what if a Christian lives in a non-Christian family, accustomed to defend itself and its property by a resort to violence, and is called upon to take part in measures of defence?" This solicitation is simply an appeal to the Christian to fulfil the decrees of truth. A Christian knows the truth only that he may show it to others, more especially to his neighbors and to those who are bound to him by ties of blood and friendship, and a Christian can show the truth only by refusing to join in the errors of others, by taking part neither with aggressors or defenders, but by abandoning all that he has to those who will take it from him, thus showing by his acts that he has need of nothing save the fulfilment of the will of God, and that he fears nothing except disobedience to that will.

"But how, if the government will not permit a member of the society over which it has sway, to refuse to recognize the fundamental principles of governmental order or to decline to fulfil the duties of a citizen? The government exacts from a Christian the oath, jury service, military service, and his refusal to conform to these demands may be punished by exile, imprisonment, and even by death." Then, once more, the exactions of those in authority are only an appeal to the

Christian to manifest the truth that is in him. The exactions
of those in authority are to a Christian the exactions of those
who do not know the truth. Consequently, a Christian who
knows the truth must bear witness of the truth to those who
know it not. Exile and imprisonment and death afford to
the Christian the possibility of bearing witness of the truth,
not in words, but in acts. Violence, war, brigandage, executions, are not accomplished through the forces of uncon-
scious nature; they are accomplished by men who are
blinded, and do not know the truth. Consequently, the
more evil these men do to Christians, the further they are
from the truth, the more unhappy they are, and the more
necessary it is that they should have knowledge of the
truth. Now a Christian cannot make known his knowledge
of truth except by abstaining from the errors that lead men
into evil; he must render good for evil. This is the life-work
of a Christian, and if it is accomplished, death cannot harm
him, for the meaning of his life can never be destroyed.

Men are united by error into a compact mass. The pre-
vailing power of evil is the cohesive force that binds them
together. The reasonable activity of humanity is to destroy
the cohesive power of evil. Revolutions are attempts to
shatter the power of evil by violence. Men think that by
hammering upon the mass they will be able to break it in
fragments, but they only make it more dense and imperme-
able than it was before. External violence is of no avail. The
disruptive movement must come from within when molecule releases its hold upon molecule and the whole mass
falls into disintegration. Error is the force that welds men
together; truth alone can set them free. Now truth is truth
only when it is in action, and then only can it be transmitted
from man to man. Only truth in action, by introducing light
into the conscience of each individual, can dissolve the ho-

mogeneity of error, and detach men one by one from its bonds.

This work has been going on for eighteen hundred years. It began when the commandments of Jesus were first given to humanity, and it will not cease till, as Jesus said, *"all things be accomplished"* (Matt. v. 18). The Church that sought to detach men from error and to weld them together again by the solemn affirmation that it alone was the truth, has long since fallen to decay. But the Church composed of men united, not by promises or sacraments, but by deeds of truth and love, has always lived and will live forever. Now, as eighteen hundred years ago, this Church is made up not of those who say *"Lord, Lord,"* and bring forth iniquity, but of those who hear the words of truth and reveal them in their lives. The members of this Church know that life is to them a blessing as long as they maintain fraternity with others and dwell in the fellowship of the son of man; and that the blessing will be lost only to those who do not obey the commandments of Jesus. And so the members of this Church practice the commandments of Jesus and thereby teach them to others. Whether this Church be in numbers little or great, it is, nevertheless, the Church that shall never perish, the Church that shall finally unite within its bonds the hearts of all mankind.

"Fear not, little flock; for it is your Father's good purpose to give you the kingdom."

BR
125
.T7132

Tolstoy, Leo, graf,
1828-1910.
The wisdom of Tolsto

FASKEN LEARNING RESOURCE CENTER

9000068941